BALL BEARINGS

D0477888

BALL BEARINGS

www.BallBearings.org

© Copyright 2003 Jeffrey Bruce Compton, Stefan Lewis Scott, Matthew Scott Tyler. All rights reserved.

No part of this publication may be reproduced, stored in a retrieval system, or transmitted, in any form or by any means, electronic, mechanical, photocopying, recording, or otherwise, without the written prior permission of the authors.

Printed in Victoria, Canada

National Library of Canada Cataloguing in Publication

Compton, Jeffrey Bruce, 1967-
        Ball bearings : the complete illustrated guide of ball exercises / Jeff Compton, Stefan Scott, Matthew Tyler.

Includes index.
ISBN 0-9732266-0-9

        1. Exercise. 2. Balls (Sporting goods) I. Scott, Stefan Lewis, 1972-
II. Tyler, Matthew Scott, 1973- III. Title.

GV484.C64 2003a   613.7'1   C2003-906996-6

First printing May 2003
Second printing December 2003

BALL BEARINGS BOOK COMPANY
www.BallBearings.org

DISCLAIMER: This book is designed for the purpose of educating the reader in regards to the subject matter covered. The information is not intended for medical diagnosis, nor should it be relied upon to recommend a treatment protocol for an individual. The authors are not responsible in any manner, whatsoever, for any injury or loss that may result following the information contained within this book. The exercises described may be too strenuous or dangerous for some people and the reader should consult their physician or other qualified health care practitioner before engaging in a new exercise regime. Never ignore medical advice or delay in seeking it because of something contained in Ball Bearings.

FOREWORD

The use of the exercise ball is more than a fad but less than a panacea. It has become one of the most popular pieces of exercise equipment in North America, appearing in clinics, fitness clubs and personal exercise rooms. Like any device, the exercise ball is open to misuse. An incorrect workout with the exercise ball can create problems. Ball Bearings provides the solution. The three authors have provided over 100 exercises, some of which have never been described in print before, and have combined their sensible, explicit instructions with practical pictures.

Jeff, Stefan and Matthew combine years of exercise training experience with the ability to teach and train clients ranging from middle-aged back pain sufferers to high performance athletes. Together they have developed an approach that addresses the exercise needs of everyone from the novice to the seasoned trainer. Ball Bearings has applications for all ages.

My professional relationship with the authors and my admiration for their talents led me to incorporate some of their basic ideas and exercises into my book A Consultation With The Back Doctor. Whether you are developing a program of spinal mobility or core stability, interested in a routine of general stretching or just familiarizing yourself with the terminology, Ball Bearings can help.

Starting on the exercise ball without reading Ball Bearings is like trying to prepare a soufflé without the recipe. You may collect all the ingredients but the results will fail to meet your expectations. Ball Bearings does not disappoint. This is a book for anyone interested in getting the most out of their time with an exercise ball.

Hamilton Hall M.D., FRCSC
Professor, Department of Surgery, University of Toronto
Co-ordinator, Spine Service, Sunnybrook and Women's College Health Sciences Centre
Medical Director, CBI Health

DEDICATION

First and foremost we would like to thank Corinne, Bianca and Kathy, for sacrificing many weekends, evenings and quality time as we worked on this project, and for the support and encouragement we received from you.

Thanks also goes to all the patients, athletes and students who have laughed at our corny jokes and put up with all of our antics.

Thanks to Dan Devlin, PT, for his technical expertise and critical eye.

We are also indebted to Dr. Werner Liedtke for his proof-reading abilities and editorial suggestions...thank you!

We are extremely grateful to Kevin Collister of Spyderbaby Productions for the endless hours of work he performed on layout and design, all the while maintaining a great demeanour... thanks Kevin!

This book is dedicated to all of you. We hope you have as much fun using it as we did in creating it!

-Jeff, Stefan & Matthew

ABOUT THE AUTHORS

JEFF COMPTON graduated with a BSc in Human Kinetics from the University of Ottawa in 1993. He has worked full time as an Exercise Therapist for over a decade. He is a Registered Kinesiologist through the British Columbia Association of Kinesiologists and a Certified Strength and Conditioning Specialist with the National Strength and Conditioning Association. As the owner of Edge Enhanced Performance Specialists, Jeff trains several of Canada's greatest athletes and presents seminars on sports specific training and injury prevention. Jeff specializes in creating and modifying ball exercises for specific needs. He has used the exercises in Ball Bearings to help a diverse range of clients from 5 to 85 years of age including those who are hearing and visually impaired, paraplegic, single and double amputee, pre and post surgical, as well as sports teams, professional athletes and world champions.

STEFAN SCOTT graduated with a BSc in Human Kinetics from the University of Ottawa in 1996. He received the University's Gold Medal for graduating at the top of his class. For the next two years he worked in rehabilitation as an Exercise Therapist. Stefan received his MSc in Sport and Exercise Science from the University of Victoria in 2000. While completing his Masters degree in Victoria, British Columbia, Stefan worked part time in rehabilitation and trained elite amateur athletes in Ice Hockey and Baseball. Stefan is currently working full time at the University of Victoria as the Senior Human Anatomy Laboratory Coordinator, teaching Introductory Human Anatomy. He also lectures part time at Victoria's West Coast College of Massage Therapy, teaching Musculo-Skeletal Anatomy and Kinesiology.

MATTHEW TYLER studied Physiology and Sports Science at Glasgow University, Scotland, graduating in 1995. He then went on to study Physiotherapy at Queen Margaret University College, Edinburgh. Matthew came to Canada for his last practicum in Victoria, BC, and graduated with his Physiotherapy degree in 1999. Since then he has continued to work in Victoria as a physiotherapist primarily treating sports and orthopaedic injuries. Matthew's patients see the benefits of the exercises in this book on a daily basis while rehabilitating many different injuries. His patients include those from the general population to elite athletes.

CREDITS

Development and Copy Editors
Jeff Compton, Stefan Scott and Matthew Tyler

Graphic Design and Layout
Spyderbaby Productions
www.SpyderbabyProductions.com

Front Cover and Back Cover Design
Greg Wiens

Spine Illustration
Willa Bradshaw

Photography
Gordon Lee
www.GordonLeePhotography.com

Ball Bearings Models
Corinne Compton
Jeff Compton
Kathy Murdoch
Matthew Tyler
Bianca Scott
Stefan Scott

Printing
Hillside Printing

Don't forget to visit our website at

www.ballbearings.org

CONTENTS

CONTENTS

C O N T E N T S

Don't forget to visit our website at
www.ballbearings.org

CHAPTER 1

Getting Your Bearings...

Ball Bearings is written for YOU. It is designed to act as your very own 'at home' Personal Trainer. Please be safe. Consult your health professional before starting or modifying your exercise program. Whenever you have questions or concerns about your health, visit your Doctor, Physiotherapist, Chiropractor, Registered Massage Therapist or Exercise Specialist. Enjoy the challenges you will undoubtedly face.

Have fun, be confident and enjoy getting your BALL BEARINGS!

WHY EXERCISE ON A BALL?

The exercise ball is a simple yet versatile tool! It has been around for a while, having made its first appearance in Europe in the early 1960's. It is sometimes referred to as a Swiss Ball, Gym Ball, Fit Ball, Physio Ball or Therapy Ball; we will refer to it as an *Exercise Ball*, or simply, a *Ball*.

No doubt you will soon notice that the Exercise Ball is 'unstable' when compared to a chair, stool, weight bench or the ground. It is this *instability* that gives the Ball its unique character and role in the world of fitness and exercise equipment.

The great advantage of this inherent instability is that it challenges your body's stabilizing muscles. The more you challenge these muscles, the stronger they become and the better they will be at keeping you stable! (Stability is discussed further on page 6)

BALL BEARINGS Can Improve Your....

Among Other Things, The Ball Is Also....

• Inexpensive - especially compared to fancy weight benches and machines! Just add air! (At time of printing, air was still free.)

• Reliable - no need to rush to the gym when you can do nearly all exercises at home. It's always ready and there for you!

• Efficient - you always exercise more than one body part. Your core (or mid-section) gets stronger as you work your arms and legs!

• Easy to care for - no maintenance or clean-up required!

• Non-Intrusive - you only need a small space... and when you're finished it is easy to roll away.

- Adaptable - the same sized ball can be used by many different people!

- Helpful - you can bounce on it or roll to the ground to get out of difficult positions!

- Portable - without the air, it can be put into a gym bag or drawer.

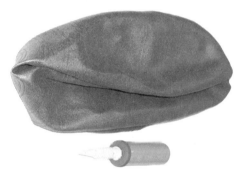

- Comfortable - changes in position are easily accommodated. You can roll into and out of lying positions, rather than falling back as you would using standard weight benches. It is also more comfortable to sit or lie on, and allows more movement of your shoulder blades.

- Versatile and Practical - it can serve as an excellent office chair, TV chair or reading support!

- Unique - Hundreds of exercises can ONLY be performed with the help of your Exercise Ball!

- Custom Fit - Adding or removing air can make it firmer/softer or more/less difficult!

- Suitable - Expert or beginner, young or old, fit or unfit - all will see benefits!

- Fun - Try to work out with the Exercise Ball without smiling...it's NOT possible!!

EGGS 'N BACK BREAKIN'

If you have ever squeezed an egg end to end, you know that it is almost impossible to break. When a force is applied, the egg remains stable.

However, if you apply a force to the egg from its side, it is unstable. What you end up with is breakfast....

In a similar fashion you can keep your spine in a stable position too. In this position, which is referred to as a NEUTRAL POSTURE, forces on your spine such as those experienced when bending, lifting, and sitting, are evenly balanced.

A Neutral Spine can be identified by three curves:

• A slight inward curve at the neck (Cervical Lordosis).

• An outward curve in the mid back (Thoracic Kyphosis), and;

• Another inward curve between your pelvis and low back (Lumbar Lordosis);

These curves combine to form the natural shape of your spine.

FRONT

Cervical Curve (Lordosis)

Thoracic Curve (Kyphosis)

Lumbar Curve (Lordosis)

WMB

NEUTRAL POSTURE

With certain activities such as sitting, standing and kneeling, your spine is prone to come out of its Neutral Posture, putting it in a more vulnerable position. With concentration we can maintain a Neutral Posture, but when stabilizing muscles become fatigued, this posture is lost.

However, with good core stability (this being one of the biggest benefits of using an Exercise Ball), you can maintain Neutral Posture for a much longer time. Since we should use our core muscles in all positions and activities, learning how to use and strengthen them not only has many advantages but also makes great sense!

Core Stabilizers Have Some UNIQUE Characteristics Compared To Other Muscles. For example:

- They are active despite positional changes, whether you sit, stand, kneel, lie face-up or face-down.

- They work to keep your body stationary or control movement while other body parts are active (i.e. jumping, lifting, throwing, pushing, pulling).

- They adapt quickly to training. Since benefits can be gained rapidly, exercises need to be adjusted frequently.

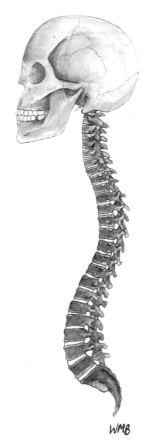

WMB

EN CORE

Starring Roles

Muscles can have two different roles. In one, they act to move the body (mobilizers), in the other they act to resist or control movement (stabilizers). In the core, the mobilizers can move you four main ways: bending forwards, backwards and sideways, as well as twisting. A well known core mobilizer is the Rectus Abdominis muscle, otherwise known as your 'Abs'. It is used when doing sit-ups. For exercises that use core mobilizers, benefits will be referred to as "improve core strength".

The role of the core stabilizers is to keep the individual bones of your spine correctly aligned while using your mobilizers. This is known as Spinal or Core Stability. These spinal stabilizers include the *Transversus Abdominis (TVA)*, *Multifidi* and *Rotatores*. To make things simple, these muscles will be referred to collectively as spinal stabilizer muscles. For exercises that use spinal stabilizers, benefits will be described as "improve core stability".

Of these three stabilizers, you can most easily

touch your TVA muscle, and therefore know when it is working. On the next page we will explain how to check for yourself if you are contracting your TVA properly.

I Just Need A Washboard Stomach!

"Sit-ups, sit-ups and even more sit-ups, that's how one gets good core strength and stability, right?" Yes and no. Washboard, yes! Core stability, no!

Sit-ups and crunches strengthen mobilizers, but even when you finally have that washboard stomach you may still have poor spinal stability. Strong mobilizers do not give you good core stability. This is because mobilizing muscles are not attached in the correct positions to do this job, and they become tired quickly.

Core Stability...So What?

Research shows that people with good core stability are less likely to suffer from lower back pain and injuries. What is the point in being able to do 200 sit-ups if your back aches for two days after pushing the lawnmower?

IS MY TVA ON?

In order to engage your TVA voluntarily and begin training it, you need to learn when it is working. This is best done with the help of a health care professional, however, the following exercise describes how to do this on your own.

Lie on your back with your knees and hips bent, feet flat on the floor. With your finger tips, find the top left and right corners of your pelvis, they should feel like hard bony points. Now slide your first two fingers down and inwards about 5 cm (2 inches). Apply moderate pressure. You are now above your TVA muscle. When relaxed it should feel soft (See TVA Relaxed next page).

To contract the TVA, hollow your lower abdomen, especially the sides, using only 20-30% of your maximum contraction. This is not as easy as it may sound. If you are having difficulty visualizing what to do or contract, try one of the prompts below for extra help.

- Imagine you have a string attached just below your belly button running through to your spine. Now pull that string towards your back bone (don't pull too hard on the string)

- Try to pull the corners of your pelvis (the hard boney points) towards each other

- Imagine pulling the sides of your waist away from your belt

If you are contracting your TVA you should feel slight tension equally under your fingertips on both sides. Remember this feeling. This is what you need to do later when you read "engage your TVA", "stabilize trunk" or "stabilize core". You will be using your TVA's a lot! (See TVA Engaged)

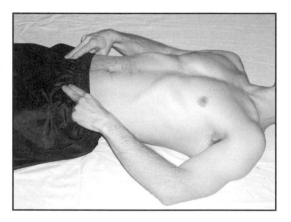

TVA Relaxed

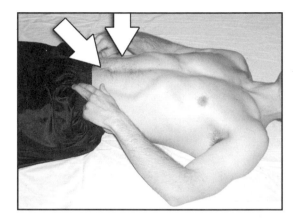

TVA Engaged

Problems? Don't Expect To Master It The First Time!

If you feel the muscles bulge up, then you are trying too hard and are starting to use your mobilizing muscles (photo 1). Back off a little. You need to learn to tighten the muscles with a low intensity effort. Postural and stabilizing muscles respond best to low forces. Keep practicing until you get it right!

You want to avoid tilting your pelvis, moving your back, breathing in and holding your breath (photo 2). If any of these happen, then you are 'cheating' by using mobilizing muscles and need more practice. If you have to use more than 20-30% of maximum effort before you feel any tension, then you still need more training of your TVA before progressing onto the Ball.

Do not worry if you have trouble doing this properly; you are not alone. Many highly trained athletes have trouble contracting their TVA properly! With repeated practice, you shoud be able to get your core stabilizers to contract on command.

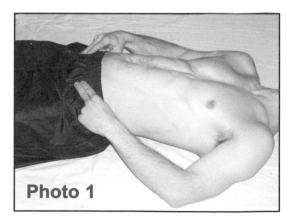

Too Much Effort: Wrong.

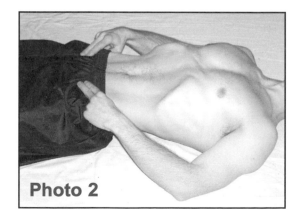

Breath Holding: Wrong.

THE BALL ESSENTIALS

Can Anyone Use The Ball?

Unfortunately, *Ball Bearings* is not suitable for people with osteoporosis due to injury risk from falling. Before starting an exercise program consult your physician. This is especially important if you are elderly; have not exercised for several months; or if you have, or suspect you may have, any medical problems.

What Ball Should I Get?

Ball Bearings strongly recommends that you purchase a burst resistant ball! These balls are typically more expensive than non-burst resistant balls. Burst resistant does not mean puncture proof. Should it be punctured, it will slowly deflate and lower you to the ground safely. The alternative? Lower quality balls can suddenly pop and you'll be dumped on the floor almost instantaneously. A valuable pointer: balls are rated on the amount of weight they can support. Choose a ball that is weight rated to support at least 500 lbs.

Smooth Vs Textured

Basically there are two types of ball surfaces: smooth and textured. One is not necessarily better than another. Typically, brands with the smooth, shiny, plastic type 'feel' are firmer, a little less bouncy, not as 'grippy' against your clothing or skin, and often have higher weight ratings - good if you classify yourself as heavy or you will be lifting heavy weights. The textured type tend to feel softer, bounce more, provide more grip, conform to your body contours better, but may not have as high a weight rating. Try them both, then get the one you like best!

Is Bigger Better?

Balls typically come in 3 diameters; 55cm, 65cm and 75cm. The best guide in choosing the right sized ball is comfort. Sit on it. You should be in a comfortable position with your knees and hips bent at approximately 90 degrees. The ball can be slightly inflated or deflated if you feel in-between sizes.

If you can't try out a ball before you buy it, a good guide is to measure the distance from your chest to your finger tips with your arm held straight out in front of you - this is most likely an appropriate size for you.

Who is "Airin DeBall"?

Not a person. We are talking about ball inflation! Your ball should be inflated approximately to its stated diameter.

An easy method to check ball height is to roll it under a desk or table. Measure the height under the table. From this, subtract the distance from the top of the ball to the table. This is the ball's diameter.

Must It Be Exact?

No. You can let some air out to adjust the firmness to suit your ability and comfort. Slightly deflating the ball makes it softer and more stable. When exercising, this is easier for beginners. Conversely, if it is fully inflated the ball will be firmer and less stable. This can test your reactions and stability a little more! However, over inflating may lead to failure of the ball below its weight rating.

Can My Ball Be Damaged?

Yes. Keep your ball away from:

- Sharp objects (jewellery, belt buckles, watches)
- Rough surfaces (rocks, gravel, sticks)
- Direct sunlight and heat sources
- Pets (dogs, cats, iguanas; but goldfish are OK :)

Can My Ball Be Repaired?

Yes, but we do not recommend this. If you suspect your ball has been damaged or if it shows visible cuts or scrapes, STOP using it. It could be close to its breaking point! Safety always comes first. Time for a new ball!

Where Should I Exercise?

Hawaii is our favourite place, but that's not what we mean. When using your ball, always exercise in a large, clear space. You could fall off. To prevent hurting anything more than just your pride, make sure you have sufficient space. This way you will not hit your head or body against anything. To reduce your risk of falling as a result of an unnecessary slip, perform exercises on a non-slip floor and wear stable footwear that grips. Carpet and linoleum floors are fine, but be sure to wear shoes on these surfaces. Avoid icy surfaces (hence Hawaii…!).

What If It Hurts To Exercise On The Ball?

The old phrase "no pain, no gain" does not apply to all situations. For the most part, pain should not be experienced when performing Ball Bearings exercises. Feelings of mild discomfort within the exercising muscles, sometimes described as 'burning', 'aching', or 'fatigue', may be felt. These sensations are similar to those in the stomach when doing many sit-ups, or in your quads when climbing a few flights of stairs. This discomfort is normal and acceptable.

Pains that are 'sharp', deep joint pains, or pain that lasts when you stop an exercise, should not be pushed through. If any of these occur, stop the exercise. Have a therapist or trainer check your technique and posture. If you cannot perform the exercise with correct technique then it is likely too advanced for you. Return to a similar, but easier exercise and then progress.

If with the correct technique you still feel pain, STOP before you injure yourself. Not all exercises are suitable for everyone. We do not all have the same bodies. A slight injury could be present. Consult a health care specialist.

Please note that some exceptions regarding pain symptoms may apply when recovering from or rehabilitating an injury. Your doctor or therapist will discuss this with you.

Can I Stand On The Ball?

Yes, but we DO NOT recommend it. Although these exercises look cool, there is too much risk of falling. It also places the feet and legs into unnatural positions. The challenges that these exercises provide can be achieved in safer ways.

Delayed Onset Of Muscle Soreness

If you are just starting to exercise, or trying a new technique, it is common to experience muscle soreness the following day. This soreness usually peaks on the second day and dissipates over the next few days. If the soreness persists for more than four to five days, tell a health care specialist.

To minimize this soreness, start your program slowly and gradually build up the amount and difficulty of the exercises.

BEARINGS ON FITNESS

Exercise: The Currency of Health

Just as you would invest money in the hopes of having that money work for you and earn a return on your investment, you must exert a certain amount of effort and energy in order to gain fitness, wellness and health. There is no magic pill that will provide you with improved muscular strength and endurance. Physical activity is the key.

Strength vs Endurance

Strength is the amount of force a muscle can generate for a specific movement. Muscular endurance is the ability to do this movement repeatedly or for a sustained period of time. A common misconception is that training muscular strength and endurance is only for athletes. This is just not true!

What's In It For Me?

Both strength and endurance are of great value to each and every one of us. We use them every day when you do house- or yard-work, walk, run, lift, carry, sit, stand or any other type of recreational activities. Increased strength and endurance makes all of these tasks easier to perform.

Strength and endurance also improves our posture, flexibility, personal appearance, self-image and increases our metabolism and energy levels. Improved strength and endurance also helps prevent low back pain, decrease risk of injury, reduce body fat, enhance the ability to recover from fatigue and improve overall quality of life! That's why the activities in *Ball Bearings* focus on training both muscular strength and endurance.

What About Power?

Power is defined as the rate at which a force is applied. For power, the question of speed of movement is important. The faster a given weight is moved, the more power is being exerted by the muscles. Power is an important concern for athletes and others in highly demanding sports or physical occupations.

However, for the majority of us, power is not that big of a concern. If you are a competitive athlete concerned about power development, please consult a Certified Kinesiologist or Exercise Physiologist for further information.

How Do I Make Gains?

In order to improve your strength and endurance, your body must be challenged to do more than usual. Tissues in the human body adapt and improve in response to the challenges they face. If muscles are required to exert more force than they are used to, they will adapt to this new level of activity by increasing their endurance and strength. This is known as the Overload Principle.

A key point to remember is that once an exercise seems easy, your muscles have adapted and become stronger. For continued improvement, challenges need to be increased.

Use It or Lose It!

The following might be called the 'Underload Principle'! If you stop challenging your muscles, they will lose the strength and endurance they have gained.

FANCY TERMS

Whole books have been written on fitness principles, exercise and training. It is not our aim to package that information into the next few pages; that's simply impossible. Our goal is to help you understand some basic fitness principles that will answer the Why's and How's of using this book.

In order to do this and get the most out of the exercises in the *Ball Bearings* book, some basic terminology needs to be discussed and understood.

Contractile Agreement?

Muscles can be either in an 'off' or an 'on' state. When they are 'off', they are relaxed. When they are turned 'on', this is known as a contraction. A muscle contraction occurs whenever a force is exerted. There are two main types of muscle contractions; Static and Dynamic:

Static Contraction

A Static Contraction takes place when muscles exert force, but their length does not change. In the photo above, a static contraction would be used to hold this position. Although the muscles are contracting, there is no movement.

Dynamic Contraction

A Dynamic Contraction results in movement or *a change in muscle length*. For repeated *Crunches* (See Figure A and B below), muscles would be performing dynamic contractions. Two distinct phases exist in a dynamic contraction: *concentric* or *eccentric*.

A Concentric Contraction exists when muscles *shorten as they produce force*. The muscles causing the movement from position A to B are shortening. In this case, the abdominal muscles are contracting 'concentrically'.

An Eccentric Contraction occurs when muscles *lengthen as they create force*. Moving from position B, back to position A, uses the same muscles, but differently. They must counteract the effects of gravity to lower the body in a controlled and safe manner. In this case the abdominal muscles are contracting 'eccentrically' (lengthening) as they exert a force.

TALKING THE TALK

Specific words that are used to describe the parameters of a workout are defined below:

Repetitions (or Reps): A repetition is one complete lifting and lowering cycle of an exercise. If you were to raise and lower yourself 10 times doing the Crunch, you would have completed 10 reps!

Set: A set consists of a certain number of repetitions performed continuously without stopping or taking any breaks. After performing your 10 continuous reps of the Crunch, you would have completed 1 set of 10 reps.

Rest Periods: This is the amount of time taken to rest in between sets of an exercise. Rest is needed between each set to allow some muscle recovery. If you do not rest, you will not be able to perform the next set effectively. Rest too long and you may not overload your muscles. Remember the Overload Principle? (See page 12)

Tempo: This is the speed at which an exercise is performed. Tempo can range from very slow to explosive. To improve general fitness, slow and controlled movements are best. A general guideline for each rep is to take two seconds to perform the concentric phase and three seconds for the eccentric phase. Remember to pause for at least one full second between concentric and eccentric phases. This should be considered a moderate tempo.

Learning The Lingo

To illustrate, let's use these terms in an example.

A

B

Your are going to perform 3 sets of 10 reps of the Hamstring Curl, with a 1 minute rest period between sets. Your course of action would be to:
• get into the start position (Figure A)
• perform 10 reps moving from position A to B at a moderate tempo
• rest for 1 minute
• repeat another 10 reps (from A to B)
• rest again (1 minute)
• repeat the final 10 reps
Voila! You have just done "3 sets of 10 reps of Hamstring Curls, with a 1 minute rest period between sets."

WALKING THE WALK

Quality...

Think about the Overload Principle again. Muscles have to be fatigued in order for them to get stronger. Therefore when you complete a set of any exercise, your muscles should be tired.

There is a fine balance here between absolute fatigue and maintaining proper technique. A general guideline is that your final repetition should be difficult, but still done with proper technique.

...and Quantity

A relationship exists between the number of reps you can do and the resistance (weight) you are moving. The lower (or lighter) the resistance, the more reps one can do. With high resistance (heavier weight), fewer reps are possible.

A perfect exercise cycle or program consisting of the 'best' number of reps, sets and rest periods does not exist. This is because each variable has a range that can be adjusted to achieve a desired outcome.

For example, to improve muscle power and brute strength, lifting very heavy weights and low repetitions are used (e.g., 1 - 5 reps). To benefit muscular endurance, lighter weights and higher repetitions (e.g., 15 - 25+ reps) should be used. Strength is gained using the range in between 5 - 15 reps. The resistance or weight used for any given exercise will determine what type of muscle improvements will be experienced.

The current fitness level also plays a role in how a body will adapt to training and overload. If you are new to exercising, improvements can be noticed quickly. Once a body becomes more fit, improvements will occur more gradually.

How Often Should I Exercise?

Frequency refers to the number of times per week a program is carried out. To *improve* muscular strength and endurance a frequency of 2 to 4 times per week is suggested. Once a fitness level is reached, it can be *maintained* with one session per week. The recommendation made as part of the *Ball Bearings* program is to aim for a frequency of 3 sessions per week.

Should I Breathe?

The question may appear trivial. It is unlikely that anyone would ever forget to breathe while exercising, but when to inhale and exhale is an important part of a successful training program! For dynamic exercises, you should inhale during the 'easier' phase, which is typically the eccentric lowering phase of a repetition. Exhaling takes place in the 'harder' lifting, or concentric phase.

Will The Ball Help My Cardio?

It is possible to enhance cardiovascular fitness while exercising with the ball. In order to challenge the heart and lungs, light resistances, higher repetitions (i.e., 20 - 40), less rest between sets (i.e., 0 - 20 seconds), and working out for at least 20 minutes at this pace are required. This is typically referred to as 'circuit training'.

Although circuit training has been shown to be beneficial, better results are obtained by performing any continuous endurance activity such as running, biking, roller-blading or cross country skiing for 20 or more minutes, 3 to 6 times per week. An intensity is required that is high enough to raise heart rate and breathing rate significantly. For more information on how to improve cardiovascular fitness, consult a health care professional.

THE BALL BEARINGS WORKOUT

Program-a-Ball!

It is possible to custom design your very own workout by following the *Program-a-Ball* key that is included with every exercise! Look for the following:

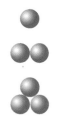

    10 times

    15 times

    20 times

Program-a-Ball is your guide. It will remind you how many of each exercise makes each set. Three categories based on different fitness level are identified: 1 ball for Beginner, 2 for Intermediate and 3 for Advanced. These categories can be used for improving general muscle strength and endurance; the type of fitness used in everyday activities.

For dynamic exercises or continuous movement, *Program-a-Ball* values tell the number of reps for each set. For static exercises, or a held contraction, *Program-a-Ball* reminds you of the time a position should be held. Repetitions, or reps, may also be indicated as follows:

    3 reps x 5 seconds

    5 reps x 10 seconds

    8 reps x 20 seconds

Sets...

The suggested number of sets that should be performed for each exercise is 3 to 5. It is recommended that 1 to 2 sets are most appropriate for those just starting to exercise, or those who have not exercised regularly for a month.

Rest Periods...

Generally it is recommended that a rest period of 45 to 90 seconds be taken between each set. For athletes, the rest period variable should be manipulated to meet the goals of a specific training cycle. Consult an Exercise Physiologist or Kinesiologist for further details.

Let's Roll!

Use the Program-a-Ball system as a guide to design your own complete workouts! Earn points based on the skill level performed for each exercise: 1 point for completing an exercise at the Beginner level, 2 points for Intermediate and 3 for Advanced. Start counting!

For a Beginner aim to earn 10 points; Intermediate 20 points, and for an Advanced 30 points! Vary your workouts by choosing at least one exercise from each of Chapters 4 through 8. Ideally each workout should consist of 8 to 12 exercises.

To get you started, examples of *Ball Bearings* workouts are provided on the following page. Once familiar with the *Ball Bearings* book, you are encouraged to design your own workouts based on your favourite exercises! Sample workout log sheets are included at the back of the book. Feel free to copy and use the log sheets to record your *Ball Bearings* workouts! Remember to exercise regularly, work hard, and most importantly...

Have Fun!!

EXAMPLE WORKOUTS

Here are 6 example workouts to help you get started. Some exercises are inherently more advanced than others, so they are grouped into Beginner, Intermediate and Advanced categories.

If you are new to exercising with a ball, try out the Beginner programs first. As you find them becoming easier, progress using the Program-a-Ball system and by trying some of the more challenging exercises!

BEGINNER 1:
1 Legged Statue
Pelvic Shimmy
The Bridge
Crunches
Back Extensions
Superman!
Wall Squats
Hamstring Curls
Chest Press
Shoulder Raise (to the Side)

BEGINNER 2:
Look Ma, No Feet!
Pelvic Tilt
Swaying Bridge
Arm Leans
Hip Crunches
The Sprinkler
Thigh Kicks
Donkey Kicks
The Swimmer
I'm Not Asleep!

INTERMEDIATE 1:
Look Ma, No Feet! Part II
Table Top
Static Push-Up
Side Bridge
Ball Squeeze
Ski Tucks
Groovy Hips
Hip Pointers
Curly Arms
Rear Shoulder Raise

INTERMEDIATE 2:
Rolling Ship
The Plank
Cossack Dancer
Windshield Wiper
Wall Side Squats
Hip-Up-Hooray
Chest Flys
Lawnmower
External Shoulder Rotation
Internal Shoulder Rotation

ADVANCED 1:
The Walkout
Iron Cross
Side Crunches
Dolphin
Ski Tuck & Twist
Lunge
Calf Raises
Push-Ups
Pullovers
Flap Your Wings

ADVANCED 2:
The Hand-Stand
Reverse Iron Cross
Kiss The Ball
Ilean
Calf Raises - Progressions
Hip Pointers Part Deux
Advanced Push-Ups
Back Shoulder Burners
The Skier
Back Spin

THE "NO EXCUSES" PROGRAM

When it seems like there is no time to exercise, the ball can still be beneficial. Use the ball as a chair while eating, watching television or working on the computer for at least 7 minutes with TVA engaged, then complete just 1 set of 4 different exercises.

You may not be 'overloading' your muscles, but this should minimize 'under loading' and strength loss.

Select 4 from:
1 legged Statue
The Walk Out
Superman
Crunches
Back Extensions
Wall Squats
The Bridge

BALL BEARINGS

Stretching

STRETCHING

Exact techniques for stretching are a frequently discussed and debated topic. A general consensus as to the best type of stretch, force applied, duration of hold or even the overall effect of the stretch does not exist. New theories and techniques are continually being developed.

Some of the more up-to-date techniques that we find most effective and use daily with clients are included in this chapter. It is not intended to suggest that this is the definitive guide to stretching, but it does provide a basic stretching program for the major muscle groups that will be exercised as part of the *Ball Bearings* program.

Why Bother?

Although aspects are still being debated, the following are considered to be the main effects and benefits of stretching:

- Improves flexibility and range of motion by lengthening muscles and connective tissues, which may decrease risk of injury

- Improves body awareness and posture

- Prevents formation of adhesions within and between muscles

- Aids in recovery of muscles when performed after a workout

- Following injury, stretching promotes correct orientation and length of new repairing tissues

Rules of Stretching

Warm-Up - muscles and connective tissue are a lot more supple when they are warm. It is recommended that prior to stretching a 5-8 minute warm-up of low to moderate intensity is carried out. This increases the circulation and temperature of exercising muscles. The warm-up may include activities such as brisk walking, marching on the spot, climbing stairs, jogging or biking.

Low Intensity- harder does not mean better. Take the stretch just past the point where you start to feel it. More tension may cause areas of microscopic damage and scar tissue formation leading to future areas of weakness and injury risk. Low intensity also promotes stretching of connective tissues (tendons, ligaments and fascia) which are more frequently injured than the muscles themselves.

One Minute Hold- no more, no less. Holding for 1 minute promotes stretching throughout the whole muscle and connective tissues. More than 1 minute should be avoided to prevent risk of trauma.

Repeat 3 Times- practice makes perfect. Repetition may help enhance muscle memory for the new length.

Order Of Stretches- stretch the whole 'chain'. Since muscles work with other muscles and are often linked with over-lapping connective tissue, stretching in sequence, i.e. calf to hamstring, to buttock, to hip, to low back, can increase the effectiveness of each stretching session.

Keep Stretches Passive-support the body area to be stretched. Unlike references in other ball books and some ball courses that are available, the stretches in this chapter do not make use of the ball. It is the opinion of the authors that stretching is most effective in a stable and supportive environment. This allows the body to be relaxed with minimal muscle and nerve activity. This cannot be achieved while balancing or leaning on a wobbling ball. Although it is not possible to make all stretches completely passive, the techniques suggested in this book attempt to minimize muscle activity as much as possible.

Don't Be Left Out!- Most of the stretches that are described are illustrated for the right side of the body. Stretches should, of course, be done for both sides.

CALF

Lean with your forearms against the wall. Put your left leg a half step forward with the knee slightly bent. Move your right leg back a half step and keep it straight. With your right heel on the ground, move your hips towards the wall until you feel the stretch in your right calf.

LOWER CALF & ACHILLES

Start in the same position as the Calf stretch but this time bend your right knee toward the floor until you feel the stretch in the heel (Achilles) area.

HAMSTRINGS

Lie on your back in a doorway or near a pillar. Lift your right leg, placing your heel against the wall with your knee slightly bent. Slide your buttocks towards the wall until you feel the stretch in middle of your right rear thigh (hamstring). If you experience any back pain with this stretch, try the modified version by bending your left knee to approximately 90 degrees.

REGULAR
(left leg straight)

MODIFIED
(left knee bent)

BUTTOCK

Lie on your back in a doorway. Bring your right knee towards your chest and place your foot on the door frame or wall. Then slide your body towards the wall until you feel the stretch in your right buttock. If you do not feel the stretch, gently pull your knee closer to your chest.

DEEP BUTTOCK

Lie on your back with your feet facing a wall. Put your right ankle just above your left knee. Bring your left knee up and place that foot against the wall. Move your body towards the wall until you feel the stretch across your right buttock region.

HIP

Stand with your right side one arm's length away from the wall. Cross your right leg behind your left. Put your body weight onto your left foot. Lower yourself towards the wall until your shoulder is leaning against it. Drop your right hip toward the wall until you feel a stretch. Keep your hips perpendicular to the wall.

QUADS

Lie on your stomach and rest your head on your left forearm. Keep your knees together and gently pull your right heel towards the buttock until a stretch is felt in the front thigh (quadriceps or 'quads'). If you experience any back pain put a thin pillow under your waist.

HIP FLEXOR

Kneel with your right knee on a pillow, left leg one stride forward with both hands on the hips. Keep your upper trunk stationary as you push your hips forward. You should feel the stretch in the front of the right hip. If not, gently arch backward. If you feel discomfort in your back, stop arching.

GROIN

Sit with your back against the wall, bend your knees and place the soles of your feet together. Gently apply pressure to the inside of your knees until you feel the stretch in your groin.

ABDOMINALS

Lie with the ball positioned under your back. Arch your back and lift your arms above your head. Be sure to relax and breathe normally. You should feel the stretch across your abdominals and trunk. If you experience any back pain, stop the stretch.

ABS (SLOPPY PUSH UP)

Lie face down on the floor. Place your elbows under your shoulders and rest on your forearms. Keep your hips on the ground as you push up with the forearms. Do not clench your buttocks. For this stretch, only hold for approximately 10 seconds, then return to the floor.

If at this level you do not feel a stretch, start with your hands under your shoulders. Again, keep hips on the ground as you push yourself up and straighten your arms. You should feel a stretch across your abdominal region. Experiencing slight pressure or tightness in your low back is normal. Do not continue with this stretch if any discomfort remains after lowering yourself down.

FOREARMS ON FLOOR   **HANDS ON FLOOR**

CHEST

Stand with your right arm raised horizontally and hand against a doorway, wall or Roman pillar. Slowly step or lean forward until you feel the stretch in you chest. Do not shrug your shoulder. Raise your arm to feel the stretch lower in your chest. Lower your arm to feel it higher in your chest. If you experience any shoulder pain stop stretching.

REAR SHOULDER

With your left hand, clasp your right elbow. Gently pull your arm across your lower chest. Do not shrug either shoulder. If you experience any pain in the front of your shoulder, stop the stretch.

BETWEEN SHOULDER BLADES

Lean against the wall with a straight back. Grasp your right wrist with your left hand. Gently pull forwards and slightly across you body until you feel the stretch between your shoulder blades. Do not shrug your shoulders.

BACK

On hands and knees, slide your hands forward along the floor. Look down, keeping your head and neck in a neutral posture. Move your buttocks back toward your heels until you feel a stretch in your upper and mid-back.

UPPER SHOULDER & NECK

In a seated position, grasp your hands behind your back. Your right hand should be behind your left buttock. Tip your head to the left shoulder without bending it forward. You should feel a stretch in your right upper shoulder and neck. If you experience left sided neck pain, stop the stretch.

NECK

In a seated position, tip your chin toward your chest. Clasp over the top of your head with the left hand. Gently pull your head to the left until you feel a stretch on the rear right side of your neck. If you experience left sided neck pain stop the stretch.

FRONT NECK

Smile and sit with your back supported and shoulders relaxed. Tilt your head to the left and then tip your chin upward by extending your neck. This stretch is more challenging than it appears. Do not be shy to ask for help with your technique. If you experience any left sided neck pain, stop stretching.

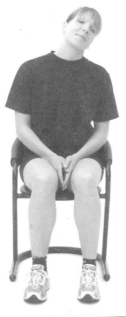

BALL BEARINGS

Balancing
the Basics

SIT ON IT!

FRONT VIEW

SIDE VIEW

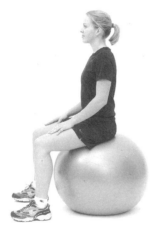

BENEFITS

Learn how to sit with correct posture on the ball with your core stabilizing muscles engaged.

TARGETS

All postural muscles involved with sitting, the lower trunk, hips and pelvis.

TECHNIQUE

Sit on the ball in a neutral position (chest out, shoulders down and back, with ears over your shoulders).

Stabilize your lower trunk by engaging your TVA (Transverse Abdominis muscle...see page 9 for explanation) and low back muscles. Keep your feet flat on the ground throughout this exercise.

Remember to keep breathing normally while you stabilize! It may be difficult at first, but do not give up!

Bearing in mind....

Unless otherwise stated, always engage your TVA and strive to maintain a Neutral Spine (Posture) while performing your exercises.

2 reps x 30 seconds

2 reps x 1 minute

3+ minutes

1 LEGGED STATUE

BENEFITS

Challenge torso and hips to maintain a neutral spine while simultaneously improving balance, muscle coordination and core stability.

TARGETS

Postural muscles, lower trunk, hips, pelvis, quads and shoulders.

FINISH

TECHNIQUE

Start seated with a neutral spine posture.

Hold your arms out to the side to help balance. Focus on stabilizing your core by contracting your TVA and lower back muscles. Be careful not to lean back while balancing.

Using a slow and controlled movement, raise one leg out in front of you and hold for a time count.

Alternate legs.

▶▶▶▶ **PROGRESSIONS**

INTERMEDIATE   **ADVANCED**

5 reps x 5 seconds

5 reps x 10 seconds

10 reps x 10 seconds

HOW TO FALL OFF YOUR BALL!

START

MIDDLE

FINISH

▶▶▶▶▶ **THE WATER SLIDE**

BENEFITS

Reduce chance of injury! Increase confidence.

TARGETS

Your body versus the floor.

TECHNIQUE

Typically, you will know when you are about to fall off your ball as your centre of gravity will have moved past the point of regaining control. You will experience the "Oh no, I'm going to fall" feeling. Remain calm.

In all seriousness, when you are about to fall off, do not try and fight it (the floor hits harder than you!). Resisting may result in a harder fall as the ball can react unfavourably to your sudden movements. Simply accept the fact that you are going to fall, go with it and roll!

Avoid putting out your arms. Instead, absorb and roll onto your shoulder or put out your foot to help break your fall. As funny as it may sound, you should actually practice falling and get a feel for how to come off the ball safely.

LOOK MA, NO FEET!

BENEFITS

Challenge balance, reaction and muscle coordination.

TARGETS

Core stability.

TECHNIQUE

Sit in a neutral posture with arms out to the side. Stabilize your lower trunk by engaging TVA and low back muscles. Keep breathing normally!

You will need to shift your weight slightly back on the ball and then slowly lift your feet off the ground. Keep your feet up without touching the floor.

START

FINISH

▶▶▶▶ **PROGRESSIONS**

INTERMEDIATE   **ADVANCED**

6 reps x 10 seconds

6 reps x 20 seconds

4 reps x 45 seconds

TOUGH TUMMY

START

FINISH

BENEFITS

Learn how to lie on the ball comfortably. The Tough Tummy is a starting position for many other exercises.

TARGETS

Abs and TVA.

TECHNIQUE

Start on your knees with your hands on the top of the ball, lean forward until your chest rests on the ball. Push with your toes, roll forward and lift your knees off the floor. As you continue to roll forward, put your hands out in front of the ball until they touch the ground.

Once comfortably balanced, focus on contracting your TVA and abdominal muscles while breathing normally. If you do not contract these muscles, the pressure of the ball on your abdomen can be uncomfortable. The goal is to maintain the contraction the whole time you are lying on the ball. Stay in your neutral spine posture!

4 reps x 10 seconds

7 reps x 10 seconds

5 reps x 20 seconds

THE WALKOUT

Increase body control in moving from a seated to lying position. The Walkout is a starting position for many exercises.

TARGETS

Low back, TVA, buttocks, hips and quads.

TECHNIQUE

Start in the neutral spine seated position. Slowly walk your feet forward while leaning back into the ball. Place your hands on the ball for added stability. Continue forward until your head rests on the ball. Keep hips up, do not sag and remember your neutral spine. In the Finish position, engage TVA but keep abs relaxed.

Try moving side-to-side and front-to-back. First time users should keep their head resting on the ball. To return to a seated position: contract your abs, bring your chin to your chest, and walk your feet back towards the ball. Even easier, from the Finish position just sit down on the ground! A great way to stretch and relax your abdominal and chest muscles is shown in the Walkout Stretch photo.

START

MIDDLE

FINISH

WALKOUT STRETCH

15 seconds

30 seconds

60 seconds

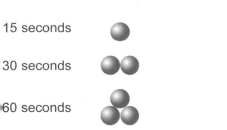

ROLLING SHIP

START

SWAY RIGHT

SWAY LEFT

▶▶▶ **PROGRESSION**

BENEFITS

Improve core stability during dynamic movements.

TARGETS

Whole trunk, buttocks, hips and quads.

TECHNIQUE

Start in The Walkout position (see previous page). With your hips, buttocks and shoulders leading the way, sway side-to-side. Do not let your hips sag and keep your trunk in a straight line from knees to head. Perform this exercise in a slow and controlled manner. Try not to get thrown overboard!

To make this exercise more challenging, hold your hands and arms straight over your head, parallel to the ground (see Progression).

15 seconds

30 seconds

60 seconds

PELVIC TILT

BENEFITS

Improve flexibility and body awareness of the lower spine and pelvis. Strengthen your lower abdominal and pelvic muscles.

TARGETS

Lower trunk musculature largely responsible for moving your pelvis and the lower abs.

TECHNIQUE

Start in a neutral sitting posture. You will be flattening your lower back by contracting your abdominal muscles (abs) and sliding your hips forward. The ball will move forward slightly as you enter the Pelvic Tilt position. Your chest, shoulders, and head should not be moving or changing their position in space.

Once you have tilted your pelvis, hold for a time count, then return to the starting position. To make this exercise even more challenging, try the One Legged Statue exercise (see page 33) while holding the Pelvic Tilt!

START

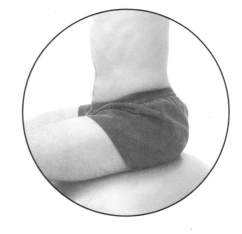

FINISH

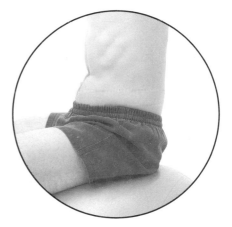

Bearing in mind....

...you will be moving out of a Neutral Spine posture while performing this exercise.

Learning how to do the Pelvic Tilt can be challenging. If you are experiencing difficulties, try the Pelvic Tilt while lying on the floor flat on your back. Place your hands under your low back. Push your back into the floor so that it flattens; you should feel pressure on your hands. Do not push with your legs, use only your abs. You are Tilting!

5 reps x 5 seconds

10 reps x 5 seconds

10 reps x 10 seconds

PELVIC SHIMMY

SIDE TO SIDE

FRONT TO BACK

BENEFITS

Improve dynamic control and range of motion of your lower trunk and hips.

TARGETS

Lower trunk including: abs, obliques (the muscles on the side of your trunk), low back and buttocks.

TECHNIQUE

These exercises take the Pelvic Tilt one step further! Start in the neutral sitting posture. The first version is to rock your hips from side-to-side (Elvis was really good at this one!).

The second version is to dynamically tilt your pelvis backwards and forwards. Your chest, shoulders, and head should not be moving or changing their position in space.

For an advanced variation, move your hips in a circular pattern to the right, back, left, and front. While in the front half of your 'circle' you will enter the Pelvic Tilt position. Keep rotating! Be sure to try it in both directions.

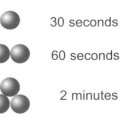

30 seconds

60 seconds

2 minutes

LOOK MA, NO FEET! PART II

BENEFITS

Challenge balance, reaction and muscle coordination.

TARGETS

Most of the muscles in your body, especially the postural ones!

TECHNIQUE

Start with two hands on the ball. There are two mounting approaches:
1. Bring one knee onto the ball, shift your body forward over the ball and bring the other knee up, or;
2. Lean both knees against the ball and shift your weight forward slowly. As the ball rolls forward, your feet will leave the ground.

Be very cautious with this exercise. Once you have your hands and knees/shins on the ball, try to balance for as long as you can. Maintain a neutral spine.

As you become better, move around side-to-side and front-to-back while balancing on the ball. This will challenge your balance and coordination even more. Progress to the kneeling position as you improve.

START

FINISH

▶▶▶▶ **PROGRESSION**

6 reps x 10 seconds

5 reps x 20 seconds

4 reps x 40 seconds

BALL BEARINGS

CHAPTER 4

Static
Body Control

THE BRIDGE

START

BENEFITS

Improve core strength and stability.

TARGETS

Hamstrings, buttocks, low back, upper back and shoulders.

FINISH

TECHNIQUE

With heels on the ball, engage your TVA and slowly raise your hips upwards until your body is straight. To help maintain balance, keep your hands out to the side, palms facing up. This adds a challenge to your upper back and shoulders.

As you get tired your hips will tend to sag; try and prevent this! However, avoid arching your hips too far towards the ceiling; do not push beyond your neutral spine position.

As you improve, bring your hands in closer to your sides. Eventually cross them on your chest. This will increase the challenge of the exercise. You can then progress to Single Leg Bridging (see Advanced).

▶▶▶▶ **PROGRESSIONS**

INTERMEDIATE	ADVANCED

5 reps x 10 seconds

7 reps x 15 seconds

8 reps x 30 seconds

SWAYING BRIDGE

BENEFITS

Improve upper back and shoulder stability.

TARGETS

Upper back, shoulders, hamstrings, buttocks, obliques and low back.

TECHNIQUE

Get into the starting position by performing The Bridge (see page 44). Once in The Bridge position, slowly sway side-to-side with your toes pointing in the direction you are swaying. Make sure you stop swaying before you reach the point of no return.

Turning your palms upwards will increase the challenge to your rear shoulder, arms, and upper back. Palms facing downwards will challenge the front of your shoulders and chest.

START

SWAY RIGHT

SWAY LEFT

20 seconds

45 seconds

90 seconds

Bearing in mind....

...coming out of the Neutral Spine position or letting your hips sag is cheating!

TABLE TOP

BEGINNER

ADVANCED

Bearing in mind....

...do not sag at the hips or overcompensate by arching your back up towards the ceiling. In the Advanced position, if you are unable to lift your leg without your buttock dropping, you need more practice at the Beginner level before advancing.

ALTERNATIVE

BENEFITS

Integrate core stability with hip strength.

TARGETS

Core, low back, buttocks, hips and quads.

TECHNIQUE

This exercise is a progression of The Walkout (see page 37). However, this time cross your arms on your chest and hold for a time count. Keep your TVA contracted and breathe normally. Remain still, avoiding side-to-side movement. Increase the challenge by lifting one leg off the ground (see Advanced). Put yourself to the test by slowly alternating legs.

First time users should keep their head resting on the ball. For the Advanced user, you can improve your neck strength by rolling back further so that your head is off the ball. Press your tongue against the roof of your mouth to engage your neck stabilizing muscles. Start slowly with this version as your neck will probably not be used to this activity! (See Alternative).

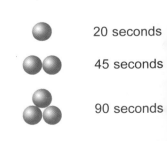

20 seconds

45 seconds

90 seconds

THE PLANK

BENEFITS

Improves whole body control.

TARGETS

Chest, quads and hips.

TECHNIQUE

This is an upside-down variation of the Swaying Bridge (see page 45).

Lie with your chest on the ball with only tip-toes on the ground. Gently hug the ball and roll it side to side. Lift your non-supporting leg into the air as you focus on keeping your spine in it's neutral posture.

You can increase the challenge by pausing at the end position before changing direction.

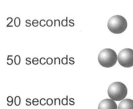

20 seconds

50 seconds

90 seconds

STATIC PUSH-UP

BEGINNER

INTERMEDIATE

ADVANCED

BENEFITS

Improve trunk and upper body strength.

TARGETS

Chest, shoulders, arms and abs.

TECHNIQUE

While kneeling, place your hands on the ball. Center your shoulder blades gently back where they are naturally placed on your body! Do not squeeze them right back or shrug them up. Keep your body and head straight, making sure not to sag. Do not lock your elbows out during this exercise. Stop if you experience shoulder pain. Hold yourself in the 'up' position for a time count.

The Static Push-Up is very challenging. Start slowly and be sure to maintain correct form at all times. If you cannot hold a neutral spine the exercise is too challenging.

If you find the Beginner version easy, place your weight onto your toes (see Intermediate photo). If this is still easy, bend your elbows slightly (see Advanced).

●   5 reps x 5 seconds

●●   5 reps x 8 seconds

●●●   5 reps x 12 seconds

THE HAND-STAND

BENEFITS

Integrate core stability with ab and upper body strength.

TARGETS

Abs, shoulders, chest, hips and quads.

TECHNIQUE

Start in the Tough Tummy position (see page 36). On your hands, slowly 'walk' forward. Keep your TVA and abs contracted. Do not let your hips sag towards the floor. Make sure you maintain a neutral spine posture. Breathe normally.

As you 'walk out' further the difficulty of the exercise will increase. Once you have walked out, hold the Hand-Stand position. Progress by only using one leg on the ball or by working your way out onto your tip-toes, or try both! (see Progressions)

If your wrists become sore in the palm flat position, try making a fist and supporting yourself on your knuckles.

START

FINISH

▶▶▶▶ **PROGRESSIONS**

INTERMEDIATE   **ADVANCED**

15 seconds

30 seconds

50 seconds

SIDE BRIDGE

START

FINISH

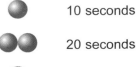

BENEFITS

Improve and integrate trunk/hip stability with strength.

TARGETS

Obliques, abs, inner and outer thigh and quads.

TECHNIQUE

From the start position, raise your hips toward the ceiling. At first you may not be able to lift your hips off the ground. This is acceptable. Simply exerting an effort will begin to strengthen your trunk. If this is too challenging try the Side Crunch on page 60.

Once you are able to raise your hips, maintain a neutral spine. You can use your hands to help balance. Do not let the ball move or let your body twist. Try to breathe normally.

Progress by balancing on your forearm. Lift your body parallel to the floor and hold.

▶▶▶▶ PROGRESSION

● 10 seconds

●● 20 seconds

●●● 40 seconds

THE BALL SQUEEZE

START

BENEFITS

Strengthen your inner thighs.

TARGETS

Inner thighs, TVA and buttocks.

FINISH

TECHNIQUE

Start in a neutral seated posture with your legs straddling the ball. Hold your hands out to the side for added balance.

Your toes should be in contact with the ground. Squeeze the ball with your inner thighs and knees. As you do this, your body will rise. Hold the Squeeze, then relax.

While you perform this exercise, try to maintain your neutral posture. To increase the challenge to your balance, close your eyes!

6 reps x 5 seconds

10 reps x 5 seconds

10 reps x 10 seconds

COSSACK DANCER

START

BENEFITS

Improve hip and leg strength.

TARGETS

Quads, buttocks, hips and abs.

FINISH

TECHNIQUE

To get into the Start position, stand back to the wall with your ball placed against the mid-back. Keep your feet about half a metre further forward. Slowly bend at the hips and knees, lowering yourself down into a 'seated' type position. Your knees should not protrude beyond the tips of your toes. Your hips, knees and ankles should all be bent to 90 degrees.

Maintain a neutral spine with your head upright. Try to keep your trunk parallel to the wall, straight up and down! Avoid letting your hips slide under the ball or towards your feet. Push against the ball to challenge the quads.

Raise one leg and hold, slowly lower, then alternate legs...now you are dancing! Place the ball higher to increase difficulty (see Progression).

▶▶▶▶▶ **PROGRESSION**

 5 reps x 5 seconds

5 reps x 15 seconds

5 reps x 30 seconds

ARM LEANS

BENEFITS

Improve shoulder/arm strength and control.

TARGETS

Shoulders, arms, chest, upper back and trunk.

TECHNIQUE

Against a wall, lean on the ball while maintaining a neutral posture. Keep your shoulder blades square to your body. Do not let them get pushed backwards, shrugged upward or roll them towards the front of your body. Hold your stance once into the leaning position. Try all three versions of the Arm Lean. They each challenge slightly different muscles.

The farther away you place your feet from the wall, the more challenging the exercise will be. Progress to using a single arm.

5 reps x 10 seconds

5 reps x 15 seconds

7 reps x 20 seconds

STRAIGHT AHEAD

UP TOP

DOWN BELOW

▶▶▶▶ PROGRESSION

IRON CROSS

FRONT VIEW

SIDE VIEW

BENEFITS

Improve stabilization of the shoulder.

TARGETS

Front shoulder, chest, arms and trunk.

TECHNIQUE

Position the ball against the wall so that your hand is at shoulder height, slightly under the centre of the ball. Stabilize your shoulder by gently pulling your shoulder blades down and back.

Place your feet so that you are leaning against the ball and are able to maintain a neutral spine. Keep your shoulders square to your body; do not let them get pushed too far backwards or roll them in front of you.

To increase the challenge of this exercise, move your feet further away from the wall.

Bearing in mind....

...this exercise can be made easier by placing the ball closer to the shoulder. This reduces elbow and shoulder strains.

3 reps x 10 seconds

5 reps x 15 seconds

6 reps x 20 seconds

REVERSE IRON CROSS

BENEFITS

Improve stabilization of the shoulder.

TARGETS

Rear shoulder, upper back, arms and trunk.

TECHNIQUE

This is similar to the Iron Cross on the previous page except now you have your back to the wall. Position the ball against the wall so that the back of your fist is at shoulder height, slightly under the center of the ball. Step away from the wall so that you are leaning backwards. Stabilize your shoulder by gently pulling your shoulder blades down and back. Your arms should be horizontal; try not to let them get pushed forward or upward.

To increase the challenge of this exercise, increase your lean by moving your feet further away from the wall.

FRONT VIEW

SIDE VIEW

3 reps x 10 seconds

4 reps x 15 seconds

5 reps x 20 seconds

BALL BEARINGS

CHAPTER 5

Dynamic Core
Mobilization

CRUNCHES

START

FINISH

▶▶▶▶ **PROGRESSIONS**

INTERMEDIATE   **ADVANCED**

BENEFITS

Increase abdominal strength and flexibility.

TARGETS

Abs and neck.

TECHNIQUE

Use the Walk Out (see page 37) to get into the Start position for Crunches. You can either cross your hands on your chest (see Start) or place your hands behind your ears to help support your head (see Intermediate). Push your tongue against the roof of your mouth to activate your deep neck muscles. With a slow and controlled pace, use your abdominal muscles to curl your upper body as if you are trying to make your chest and belly button meet, rising up until your shoulder blades come off the ball. Pause for a second, then slowly return to the Start position and repeat.

Do not bounce on the ball or use the ball to 'rebound' yourself back up. You must keep your low back in contact with the ball at all times. The ball should not move during this exercise. Progress by rolling yourself further back over the ball to start.

 8 times

 15 times

 30 times

HIP CRUNCHES

BENEFITS

Increase lower trunk strength and control.

TARGETS

Lower abs, pelvis and front of hips.

TECHNIQUE

With knees bent, squeeze the ball between your legs. Without changing knee angle, use your hips to lift your legs towards your chest. Hands can be used palms up for support.

The Progression requires a high level of core and abdominal strength. You may be at risk for injury if you cannot perform this exercise with excellent technique. To check that you are performing this Hip Crunch correctly, keep your finger tips under your low back. If upon lowering your legs you feel your low back lift off your finger tips, STOP! You are no longer in a neutral spine position. If this is the case, lower your legs only to point where your low back is about to lift, pause, and return to the Start position. With practice and increased core strength you will be able to lower your legs farther and farther.

FINISH

▶▶▶▶ **PROGRESSIONS**

START   **FINISH**

10 times

15 times

25 times

SIDE CRUNCHES

START

FINISH

▶▶▶▶ **PROGRESSION**

BENEFITS

Increase lateral trunk strength.

TARGETS

Obliques, abs and outer hips.

TECHNIQUE

Perform Side Crunches with your feet against a wall. Your technique will be much better this way. Put your hip onto the ball. Ensure that the ball is under you hip and not your ribs! Place your hands on the ball for additional balance and support. You are now in the Start position.

Keep your trunk perpendicular to the floor; do not twist. Crunch up sideways using the muscles on the topside of your trunk. If you cannot raise yourself up very high at first, do not be discouraged. You are still challenging and strengthening your muscles by contracting them. Alternate sides.

Progress by crossing hands over your chest or behind your head.

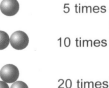

● 5 times

●● 10 times

●●● 20 times

S U P E R M A N !

BENEFITS

Improve back strength and stability.

TARGETS

Low, mid, and upper back, buttocks, shoulders and abs.

FINISH

TECHNIQUE

Start in the Tough Tummy position (see page 36) with the ball under your hips and abdominal region. Slowly raise one arm and the opposite leg.

The goal is to avoid side-to-side movement, as well as twisting hips and upper back. Do not lift your limbs so high that either your hip or shoulder rotates and causes you to lose your neutral posture. You can test this by balancing an object like a golf club across your back while performing the exercise. The golf club should not tip or dip to either side.

Progress by trying to lift three limbs at once...is it a bird?...Is it a plane?...

▶▶▶▶ **PROGRESSION**

5 reps x 5 seconds

8 reps x 10 seconds

8 reps x 15 seconds

BACK EXTENSIONS

START

BENEFITS

Improve low back strength.

TARGETS

Low and mid back, as well as buttocks (if you contract them).

FINISH

TECHNIQUE

Start in the Tough Tummy position (see page 36) with the ball under your hips and lower abdominal region. Your feet should remain on the floor the whole time. Should your feet start slipping too much, place them against a wall. If you are new to this exercise, you may place your hands on the ball for balance. The low back should be doing the work, not your arms.

Using a slow and controlled pace, arch your back by raising your chest up and away from the ball. Pause briefly at the top. Slowly return to the Start position and repeat. No bouncing! Your head and neck should remain in a neutral posture.

Progress by placing hands behind your head and increasing repetitions.

▶▶▶▶ PROGRESSION

10 times

15 times

30 times

DOLPHIN

START

BENEFITS

Improve low back strength.

TARGETS

Low back, buttocks and hamstrings.

FINISH

TECHNIQUE

Start in the Tough Tummy position (see page 36) with the ball under your hips. Raise your legs so that your whole body is horizontal. Elbows should not be locked. Keep them slightly bent at all times. It you feel wrist pain, make fists and balance on your knuckles.

Now, lift your heels toward the ceiling, squeezing your buttocks and feet together as you move. Use a slow and controlled movement, do not whip your legs up. A common technique error with the Dolphin consists of having the upper body dip downwards as the legs rise. Try to avoid this! Your upper body should remain still throughout the exercise.

Your low back will move out of the neutral spine position during this exercise. However, keep your neck in its neutral posture as shown in the illustrations.

8 times

12 times

20 times

Bearing in mind....

...ensure TVA control.

KISS THE BALL

START

BENEFITS

Increase trunk and upper body strength.

TARGETS

Abs, TVA, chest and shoulders.

FINISH

TECHNIQUE

In a kneeling position, lean on the ball with your forearms. Maintain a neutral spine, straightening your arms to move the ball forward. Breathe normally and control the movement. Stop your roll out before your back and hips start to 'sag' towards the floor.

Once your body is stretched out as far as possible, pull yourself back to the Start position by drawing your elbows toward you. Keep practicing and see if you can eventually Kiss The Ball!

It is very easy to adjust the difficulty of this exercise. By starting with the ball farther away from you, the challenge will be increased. Stop the exercise if you feel any shoulder pain or instability.

▶▶▶▶ **PROGRESSION**

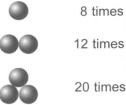

8 times

12 times

20 times

THE SPRINKLER

BENEFITS

Improve dynamic control and range of motion of core and shoulder muscles.

TARGETS

Core, obliques and shoulders.

TECHNIQUE

Start in the Table Top position (see page 46). With elbows slightly bent, raise the weight over your chest. Rotate your upper trunk to the left and keep the weight directly in line over your chest. Return to the Starting position. Repeat to the right.

Keep the weight directly in line over your chest as your rotate throughout this exercise. Your belly-button should always be facing the ceiling. For the advanced version, attempt by balancing on one leg only!

START

LEFT

RIGHT

▶▶▶▶ **PROGRESSION**

8 times

12 times

20 times

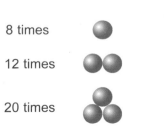

SWAYING BRIDGE II

START

BENEFITS

Improve core mobilization and stability.

TARGETS

Obliques, outer hips, hamstrings, buttocks and low back.

LEFT

TECHNIQUE

This exercise appears quite similar to its namesake, the 'Swaying Bridge' (see page 45). However, with this version, you will definitely feel the challenge shift to your outer hips and oblique muscles. Get into the Start position by performing The Bridge (see page 44). From this position lead with your heels pointing outwards as you slowly sway back and forth. Allow your outer hip to rotate and rise up as you sway towards the 'point of no return' (but not beyond it)!

Keep your palms face up to challenge to your rear shoulder, arms, and upper back. Palms face down to challenge the front shoulder and chest.

RIGHT

- 20 seconds
- 40 seconds
- 60 seconds

WINDSHIELD WIPER

BENEFITS

Improve core stability, strength and range of motion.

TARGETS

Obliques, outer hips, hamstrings, buttocks and low back.

TECHNIQUE

Lie on your back. With knees and ankles bent at 90 degrees, place your heels on the ball. Keep your arms on the floor away from your sides, palms up. Rotate both legs together to one side. Go as far as you can before a shoulder loses contact with the floor. Return to the top and repeat to the other side.

To increase difficulty, perform with only one leg on the ball and the other pointed up to the ceiling.

5 times

10 times

15 times

START

LEFT

RIGHT

SIDE VIEW

SKI TUCKS

START

BENEFITS

Increase abdominal strength.

TARGETS

Abs, shoulders, arms and front of hips.

FINISH

TECHNIQUE

Start in the Hand-Stand Finish position (see page 49). Contract your abs to bring knees towards your chest. Focus on contracting maximally throughout the movement.

During this exercise keep a neutral neck posture. Do not let your back sag nor lock your elbows; keep them slightly bent.

To increase the challenge of Ski Tucks, start with the ball positioned closer to your feet (see Intermediate photo). Now only your toes will be in contact with the ball for the Finish position. Once you have mastered the two legged approach, try it with only one. Good luck!

▶▶▶▶ PROGRESSIONS

INTERMEDIATE   ADVANCED

5 times

10 times

20 times

S K I   T U C K   &   T W I S T

BENEFITS

Increase trunk rotational strength and whole body control.

TARGETS

Abs, obliques, shoulders, arms and hips.

TECHNIQUE

Start in the Ski Tucks Finish position (see previous page). Once in this position, keep your abs contracted and slowly rotate your trunk over to one side. Your uppermost shin will lift off of the ball, with the downward shin now bearing the weight.

Challenge yourself by lowering your hips as far as possible to the sides. Do not lock your elbows. Keep your knees and ankles together.

Increase the challenge by starting with the ball positioned under your feet.

START

LEFT

RIGHT

5 times

10 times

15 times

STANDING FIGURE 8's

START

BENEFITS

Integrate the use of core stabilizers with arm movement.

TARGETS

Shoulders and postural muscles involved with standing and twisting.

TECHNIQUE

Stand in the 'power position': Hips, knees and ankles moderately bent, spine in a neutral position. Engage your TVA and low back muscles. Move the ball in a figure 8 shape, but try not to allow your trunk to twist or bend. You can 'Draw' other figures if you wish…except for a number 1…

Bearing in mind....

…the 'power position' is one using 'neutral posture' with knees bent and feet shoulder width apart.

20 seconds

45 seconds

90 seconds

ILEAN

BENEFITS

Increase lateral trunk and shoulder strength.

TARGETS

Abs, obliques, shoulders and arms.

TECHNIQUE

In a kneeling position, lean sideways onto the ball with your elbow. In a neutral spine, slowly let the ball roll away as you lean farther over to that side.

To return to the Start position pull your elbow back towards your side. Be sure to look as miserable as possible throughout the whole exercise!

FINISH

5 times

10 times

15 times

BALL BEARINGS

Lower Body
Strength

THIGH KICKS

START

FINISH

BENEFITS

Integrate leg strength with core stability.

TARGETS

Quads, TVA, inner thigh and hips.

TECHNIQUE

Place finger tips under your low back and squeeze the ball between your ankles. With hips bent at 90 degrees, slowly straighten your knees to lift the ball. Return to the Start position. Keep your head resting on the floor so that your neck remains relaxed.

Maintain a neutral spine throughout this exercise. If you feel increased pressure from your back against your fingertips, then you are cheating and using your abs instead of your TVA. If you feel your back lift off your finger tips you are not stabilizing your low back and should practice easier exercises to strengthen your TVA, such as the Hand-Stand on page 49.

5 times

12 times

20 times

WALL SQUATS

BENEFITS

Integrate leg strength with core stability; great for improving lifting technique!

TARGETS

Quads, hips, buttocks and TVA.

TECHNIQUE

Lean on the ball and place your feet one step in front of you. Slowly lower into a 'seated' position so that your trunk is parallel to the wall and at right angles to your thighs. Avoid letting your buttocks slide under the ball or towards your heels! Pause for a second before returning to the Start position.

In the Finish position, your knees should not protrude beyond the tips of your toes. When straightening your legs, do not let your knees 'snap' back. Move in a controlled manner, maintain a neutral posture, and keep your head upright throughout.

Progress by using only one leg, starting with the ball higher up on the wall, holding weights, or all three!

START

FINISH

▶▶▶▶ **PROGRESSION**

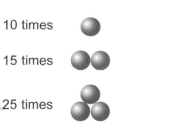

10 times

15 times

25 times

GROOVY HIPS

START

1

2

3

4

BENEFITS

Improve dynamic balance and lower body strength.

TARGETS

Quads, buttocks, hips and trunk.

TECHNIQUE

This is similar to the Wall Squat (previous page) but with a new groove!

Instead of squatting straight up and down, move your hips in a circular fashion, out to one side as you squat down and then to the opposite side as you straighten up. Perform this exercise in both clockwise and counter-clockwise directions.

Bearing in mind....

...circle with your hips only; keep your upper- and mid-back in the neutral spine position.
A common error is for the circular motion to occur at your knees. Try not to let this happen! Think hips, hips, hips!

 10 times

 15 times

25 times

WALL SIDE SQUATS

BENEFITS

Improve leg strength and trunk control.

TARGETS

Quads, outer hips, buttocks and trunk.

TECHNIQUE

Standing sideways to the wall, lean against the ball with your shoulder. Do not bend at the waist; keep your body straight. While stabilizing your trunk, slowly lower yourself down and up. Your outer leg will bear most of your weight.

To progress, perform the exercise standing only on your outside leg. For a greater challenge, increase your leaning angle! You can also try this standing on the inside leg only.

START

FINISH

▶▶▶ **PROGRESSIONS**

ONE-LEG:

START   **FINISH**

10 times

15 times

25 times

LUNGE

START

FINISH

BENEFITS

Improve balance, lower trunk stability and lower body strength.

TARGETS

Quads, buttocks and hips.

TECHNIQUE

With hands on hips, bend your knee and place the top of one foot on the ball behind you. If your shin is on the ball, you need to increase the distance between the ball and your front foot. Lower down until you feel a stretch in the front hip of your rear leg. Raise yourself back to the Start position.

Try not to lean forward, keep your upper body in a neutral posture and perpendicular to the floor at all times. This is one of the trickiest parts to this exercise!

To challenge your balance more, try it with your eyes closed. For increased strength, hold weights in your hands.

Bearing in mind....

...your knee should not move past your toe in the Finish position. If it does, you need to move the foot forward to reduce strain on your knee joint.

5 times

10 times

20 times

CALF RAISE

BENEFITS

Increase lower leg strength and balance, as well as core stability.

TARGETS

Calves and low back.

TECHNIQUE

Stabilize your trunk throughout the Calf Raise exercise. Raise yourself up and down on your tip-toes while leaning back on the ball. Move through a full range of motion and avoid locking your knees.

For the Beginner version, place the ball between your back and the wall. To progress, move your feet farther away from the wall. This will put an increased demand on your trunk.

FINISH

10 times ⬤

20 times ⬤⬤

30 times ⬤⬤
⬤

CALF RAISE-PROGRESSIONS

START -INTERMEDIATE

FINISH

BENEFITS

Challenge calf muscles through a greater range of motion.

TARGETS

Calves, TVA and abs.

TECHNIQUE

For the Intermediate and Advanced Calf Raises, you will be facing the wall with your chest on the ball. Use your TVA to stabilize your spine. Rise up and down on your tip-toes and have your heels gently touch the ground with each repetition.

Progress by moving your feet further away from the wall. For the Advanced version, perform the Calf Raises on one leg. Remember to exercise both legs.

▶▶▶▶ **PROGRESSION**

ADVANCED

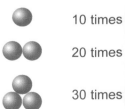

10 times

20 times

30 times

HAMSTRING CURLS

BENEFITS

Improve leg strength and core stability.

TARGETS

Hamstrings, trunk, buttocks and hips.

TECHNIQUE

The Start position for the Hamstring Curl is similar to the Finish position of The Bridge (see page 14). But this time your heels will be on the ball.

For beginners, keep your hips and buttocks a little closer to the floor and at a constant height throughout the exercise. Using your heels, pull the ball towards your buttocks maintaining a neutral spine. When returning to the Start position, move slowly and do not lock your knees at the end.

To progress, raise your hips up towards the ceiling as you pull the ball beneath you and cross arms on chest (see Intermediate). Then try it with a single leg! (see Advanced).

START

FINISH

▶▶▶▶▶ **PROGRESSIONS**

INTERMEDIATE   **ADVANCED**

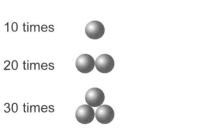

10 times

20 times

30 times

DONKEY KICKS

START

BENEFITS

Increase core strength/stability and improve the mechanics of hip movement.

TARGETS

Buttocks, hips, low back, TVA and abs.

FINISH

TECHNIQUE

Start this exercise in the Tough Tummy position (see page 36). Once in this position, engage your TVA and move yourself over to one side. Only half of your stomach and chest will remain on the ball (see Posterior View). You will need to use your outer arm to help stabilize and balance yourself.

Once you are in the Start position, extend your outer leg backwards. Try not to extend so far back that your hips rotate! Both the hips and low back should remain in a neutral posture. Try placing a wooden dowel or a golf club across your low back; keep it steady as you do your Donkey Kicks! It should not roll, dip or swing.

Increase the challenge by adding ankle weights or using a pulley or elastic tubing in the gym.

POSTERIOR VIEW

 10 times

15 times

20 times

STRIDERS

BENEFITS

Engage core stabilizers and strengthen hip muscles.

TARGETS

Buttocks, hip, quads, hamstrings and core.

TECHNIQUE

Stand with one foot on the floor in front of the ball. Place the sole of your back foot on the ball. This foot should be turned somewhat outward. Keep knees slightly bent and engage your TVA to maintain a neutral spine. Push the ball back, pointing your toe at the end of the movement. Pull the ball back towards you, rolling onto the sole of your foot into the Start position once more.

Keep your shoulders square and look straight ahead during this exercise.

START

FINISH

10 times

15 times

25 times

ZZ BOTTOMS

START

1

2

3

4

BENEFITS

Engage core stabilizers in a standing position while moving your legs.

TARGETS

Postural and pelvic muscles used in standing and twisting.

TECHNIQUE

Stand behind the ball with one foot on the floor as you place the other on the ball. Keep your knees slightly bent and spine in a neutral posture. Stabilize your trunk by engaging your TVA. Roll the ball repeatedly in a 'Z' motion by straightening and bending your hip and knee.

Do not allow your trunk to twist or bend; keep it stable.

5 times

12 times

20 times

KNEE UPS

BENEFITS

Improve hip/pelvis stability and strength.

TARGETS

Outer hip, outer thigh, and buttocks.

TECHNIQUE

Place the ball between the wall and your outer knee. You are now standing on your outer-most leg. Bring the ball towards the chest by raising your knee. Lower your knee and ball back towards the floor.

There are two versions of this exercise. For the Knee version, as you raise your thigh, simultaneously push the ball against the wall with your knee. This targets your outer hip/thigh. For the Ankle version, push on the ball with your ankle as you bring your knee up. This will strengthen your inner thigh/hip muscles.

KNEE VERSION

ANKLE VERSION

8 times

12 times

20 times

HIP POINTERS

INNER THIGH

START

FINISH

OUTER THIGH

START

FINISH

BENEFITS

Increase dynamic and static hip strength; challenge balance.

TARGETS

Inner and outer hips, obliques.

TECHNIQUE

Lie with your side on the ball, using your hand to help balance. For the Inner Thigh, lift and lower your bottom leg as high as you can; it should be in front of your supporting, or top, leg.

For the Outer Thigh, lift and lower your top leg as high as possible. You will need to shift your supporting, or lower leg, back somewhat to help balance yourself.

For both versions, keep your pelvis perpendicular to the floor. Train both sides of your body. You can increase the challenge by adding ankle weights.

For a more strenuous hip exercise...see the next page!

 8 times

 15 times

25 times

HIP-UP-HOORAY

BENEFITS

Increase dynamic and static hip strength.

TARGETS

Inner and outer hips.

TECHNIQUE

Begin in a side lying position with the ball gripped between your ankles. Use one hand as a pillow and the other to assist your balance. Without twisting at the pelvis, raise your legs as high as you can, then bring them down.

Do not forget to perform Hip-Up-Hooray lying on both your right and left side.....and try not to drop the ball!

START

FINISH

8 times

15 times

20 times

Bearing in mind....

...emphasize TVA control.

HIP POINTERS PART DEUX

INNER THIGH

START

FINISH

OUTER THIGH

START

FINISH

BENEFITS

Integrate hip and core strength with balance and stability.

TARGETS

Inner/outer hips and trunk.

TECHNIQUE

Assume the Start position for the Side Bridge (see page 50). You may use your arm and hand for balance. For the Inner Thigh, bridge with your upper leg and then slowly lift and lower your bottom leg in front of the supporting leg.

For the Outer Thigh, bridge up onto your lower leg before slowly lifting and lowering your top leg. Keep the top leg in front of your supporting leg. Now flip over and repeat on the other side.

This is an Advanced exercise. If you are unable to perform it with good technique you probably still require more training of your core strength and overall balance. Practice the Side Bridge exercise further. If you experience discomfort, bring the ball closer to your knee.

3 times

5 times

10 times

STANDING CHINS

BENEFITS

Improve upper body strength, knee and hip stability.

TARGETS

Upper back muscles, quads, buttocks, calves, shoulders and arms.

TECHNIQUE

This exercise involves holding leg contractions at various angles to help improve hip, knee and ankle stability. Grip a chin-up bar tightly with palms facing forward. Place one foot on the top of the ball. Pull yourself up towards the bar with your arms while lightly pushing into the ball with your legs. Ensure that your knee and hip are stable with muscles contracted. Avoid jerky and sudden movements

Gradually take some weight off the foot on the ground until you can lift it off completely. For the leg on the ball, hold your hip and knee in a stable static contraction at various angles for a time count.

START

FINISH

3 reps x 5 seconds

5 reps x 8 seconds

8 reps x 12 seconds

BALL BEARINGS

Upper Body
Strength

PUSH UPS

START

FINISH

▶▶▶▶ PROGRESSIONS

START   FINISH

BENEFITS

Improve upper body strength and shoulder stability. Great for improving neutral spine posture during pushing activities.

TARGETS

Triceps, chest, shoulders and trunk.

TECHNIQUE

You need good static trunk strength to perform this exercise (see Static Push Up on page 48). The key is to maintain a strong neutral spine throughout the exercise. Stabilize your trunk by contracting your TVA and abs.

Kneel on the floor, with your hands on the ball a little wider than shoulder width apart. To shift the challenge away from your chest and more to your triceps, place your hands closer to each other. This will also provide a greater challenge to your balance. Slowly lower your chest towards the ball until you are almost touching. Push yourself back up, exhaling while you do so.

To progress, straighten your legs and balance on your toes (see 'Progressions').

5 times

10 times

20 times

CHEST PRESS

BENEFITS

Integrate balance and back stability while increasing upper body strength.

TARGETS

Triceps, chest, low back and shoulders.

TECHNIQUE

For this exercise you will be holding weights in your hands as you get into the Table Top position. As you lower and roll into this position, keep the weights close to your chest. From the Start position, press the weights up until they almost touch above your chest (see Finish photo). Palms face forward at all times. Next, slowly lower the weights. Keep your forearms in a vertical position, pointing straight up to the ceiling throughout the exercise.

A common error consists of arching your hips and low back up or letting them sag as fatigue sets in. Focus on maintaining a neutral spine at all times! To progress, increase the weight and/or repetitions.

FINISH

10 times

15 times

20 times

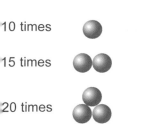

CHEST FLYS

START

BENEFITS

Improve upper body and low back strength.

TARGETS

Chest, shoulders, trunk and biceps.

FINISH

TECHNIQUE

Use The Walkout (see page 37) to get into the Start position. Hold the dumbbells with palms facing each other. This shifts the focus towards your chest muscles instead of targeting your triceps.

Remember to stabilize your trunk and not let your hips sag. Keep your elbows in a slightly bent position and lower your arms in a wide arc. You should feel a gentle stretch in your chest when the weights are at their lowest position. Now bring your hands back together.

To progress, increase the weight and/or the repetitions.

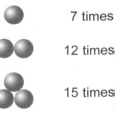

7 times

12 times

15 times

PULLOVERS

BENEFITS

Integrate upper body strength with core stability.

TARGETS

Chest, shoulder, arms, buttocks and trunk.

TECHNIQUE

Get into the Start position using The Walkout (see page 37). Keep your TVA, buttocks and hips contracted. Grip the weight with both hands. Slowly lower the weight down and behind your head with a slight bend in your elbows. Stop when you feel a slight stretch in your chest and shoulders. Exhale as you raise the weight back up to the Start position. Repeat.

Increase the challenge, and your strength, by increasing the reps and/or the weight.

START

FINISH

7 times

10 times

15 times

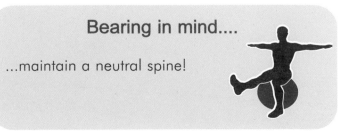

Bearing in mind....

...maintain a neutral spine!

THE SWIMMER

START

BENEFITS

Integrate upper body strength with core stability.

TARGETS

Chest, shoulder, arms, buttocks and trunk.

TECHNIQUE

This is similar to Pullovers on the previous page, but the range of arm motion is increased. Engage your TVA and buttocks; keep your hips up. Hold the weights above your chest, palms facing each other in the Start position.

Lower one arm in an arc above your head while the other arm arcs down to your hip. Let your arms rotate as you move them; both palms should finish in a face up position. Finish with arms parallel to the ground, then reverse the movement. Keep elbows slightly bent.

7 times

12 times

15 times

ADVANCED PUSH UPS

BENEFITS

Improve upper body strength, shoulder and core stability.

TARGETS

Triceps, chest, shoulders, trunk and abs.

TECHNIQUE

Assume the Advanced Hand Stand position (see page 49). Keep your nose pointed at the floor throughout this exercise to ensure good head posture. Once you are balanced, slowly lower your chest until your nose almost touches the ground. Pause, then push up.

A narrow hand placement puts more load on triceps, while a wider placement emphasizes the chest muscles.

Progress by keeping only one foot on the ball!

START

FINISH

Bearing in mind....

...your body should be straight with a neutral spine. If you start sagging at the hips or experience shoulder pain, stop the exercise.

5 times

10 times

15 times

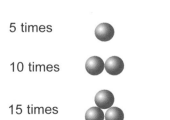

▶▶▶▶ **PROGRESSIONS**

START   **FINISH**

CURLY ARMS

START

FINISH

BENEFITS

Integrate arm strength with postural control.

TARGETS

Biceps and core.

TECHNIQUE

Another exercise that challenges your postural abilities. All those exercises from Chapters 2 and 3 will benefit you now!

Start in a seated position. Grip the weights with relaxed arms at your sides, palms facing forward. Completely lift one weight up to your shoulder, then fully lower it. Repeat the same motion with the opposite arm. The ball should not move during this exercise. Try to maintain a neutral posture by contracting your core stabilizers.

For a greater challenge to the postural muscles, lift both arms at the same time, but do not allow your trunk to sway or lean backwards. To increase the challenge to your biceps, use a heavier weight, or perform more reps.

10 times

15 times

20 times

FLAP YOUR WINGS

BENEFITS

Strengthen upper back and shoulders. Improves upper back and shoulder posture.

TARGETS

Upper, mid, and low back; neck and shoulders.

TECHNIQUE

Use the Tough Tummy (see page 36) to prepare to Flap Your Wings! Your head and neck should be aligned in their neutral posture. With your elbows slightly bent, raise your arms upwards. Focus on gently squeezing your shoulder blades together as the arms approach their highest position. Pause for a moment, then slowly lower your arms back down to the Start position.

Remember to exhale when raising the arms up, inhale as you lower them. Be careful not to shrug the shoulders up towards your ears. To progress, use weights and/or increase the reps. Remember to increase the weight as the exercise becomes easier.

START

FINISH

 **PROGRESSION**

10 times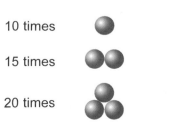

15 times

20 times

I'M NOT ASLEEP!

START

BENEFITS

Strengthen upper back, neck, and postural muscles. Increase shoulder range of motion.

TARGETS

Upper and mid-back, neck and shoulders.

FINISH

TECHNIQUE

Similar to Flap Your Wings (previous page), however, this exercise is a little more challenging and shifts the focus to your shoulders. Get into the Start position using the Tough Tummy (see page 36). Your head and neck should be aligned in their neutral posture, with nose pointed to the floor.

Raise one arm upward, straight in front of your head. Focus on keeping your shoulders and upper back parallel to the floor. If you cheat or raise your arm too high, your shoulders and upper back will 'rock' side-to-side. Try to avoid this! Slowly lower your arm back down, pause, then alternate and raise your other arm.

Progress with weights and by increasing reps.

▶▶▶▶ PROGRESSION

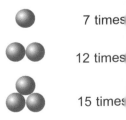

7 times

12 times

15 times

REAR SHOULDER RAISE

BENEFITS

Improve upper back postural control and rear shoulder strength.

TARGETS

Shoulder, upper back and triceps.

TECHNIQUE

Use the Tough Tummy (see page 36) to position yourself. Hold shoulder blades slightly down and back. Maintain a neutral posture. The ball should remain motionless throughout this exercise.

Raise the weights up slowly towards the ceiling, leading with your pinkies. Keep elbows slightly bent. Move the weights past your buttocks or as far as you can within a pain-free range. Exhale as you do so. Pause for a moment then lower the weights. Increase the weight to progress.

START

FINISH

7 times

12 times

15 times

LAWNMOWER

START

FINISH

BENEFITS

Strengthen back and improve core stability for bent over postures and pulling activities.

TARGETS

Upper and mid back, as well as rear shoulder and arm.

TECHNIQUE

With left foot forward and right foot back, place your left hand on the ball (or do the hookie-pookie!). Bend at the hips and knees to keep your back parallel with the floor as you gently lean onto the ball.

Exhale as you pull your elbow towards the ceiling. The weight should just touch your lower ribs. Focus on squeezing your shoulder blade down and back at the Finish position. Slowly lower the weight and drop your shoulder down at the end of the movement. Do not twist at the trunk.

To make this exercise more challenging, stand on the balls of your feet throughout the movement!

8 times

12 times

15 times

SHIFTY SHOULDER

BENEFITS

Improve shoulder stabilization, range of motion and posture.

TARGETS

Shoulder and upper back.

TECHNIQUE

Place hand face down on the ball. Adjust body position so that your hand and shoulder are at the same height. You may have to kneel and/or place the ball on a table or stool.

With a straight arm, pull your shoulder blade back and downward. Do not let your elbow bend, this is cheating. Pause, then reach forward until you feel a stretch in the shoulder blade region. Maintain a downward pressure on the ball throughout this exercise.

SHOULDER BACK

SHOULDER FORWARD

10 times

15 times

20 times

Bearing in mind....

...this movement is subtle, there should be no movement or rotation of the trunk.

EXTERNAL SHOULDER ROTATION

START

FINISH

BENEFITS

Strengthen Rotator Cuff muscles and increase shoulder stability.

TARGETS

Shoulder and upper back.

TECHNIQUE

Use the technique described in Side Crunches (page 60) to get into the Start position. To target only the rotator cuff muscles, keep your elbow bent at 90 degrees at all times. Hold your shoulder blade gently down and back as the weight reaches its uppermost position. Move through a pain free range.

To ensure your technique is appropriate, have someone watch you. Keep your upper arm 2 inches from your side. You can place a pillow or rolled towel under your elbow and slightly squeeze in. It should be 'pivoting' around the point of your elbow. Only your forearm and hand should move.

Bearing in mind....

Many of the preceding shoulder exercises have used the Rotator Cuff muscles in their role as shoulder stabilizers. This exercise and the next specifically targets them as mobilizers.

 7 times

10 times

 15 times

INTERNAL SHOULDER ROTATION

BENEFITS

Strengthen Rotator Cuff muscles and increase shoulder stability.

TARGETS

Shoulder and upper back.

TECHNIQUE

This exercise is a partner to External Shoulder Rotation on the previous page.

Assume the Start position. Keep your elbow bent at 90 degrees. The point of your elbow should remain slightly in front of your torso, and in the same position throughout the exercise. Do not lie on your arm. This position isolates the rotator cuff muscles. Very slowly raise the weight up and across your abdomen, towards the opposite elbow. Move through a pain free range.

Have someone watch and provide feedback on your technique.

START

FINISH

10 times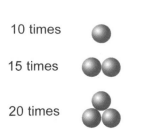

15 times

20 times

BACK SHOULDER BURNERS

START

FINISH

BENEFITS

Increase shoulder strength and improve upper back posture.

TARGETS

Rear shoulder and upper back.

TECHNIQUE

Back Shoulder Burners places the challenge on to the large rear shoulder muscles as opposed to the rotator cuff. Now you will be moving your whole arm and shoulder, not just your forearm.

Start with your arm positioned across your lower chest and the shoulder blade slightly rolled forward. Maintaining a slight bend in your elbow, raise the weight upward in a large arc. Simultaneously draw your shoulder blade back. Lower the weight slowly and repeat.

●   7 times

●●   10 times

●●●   12 times

SHOULDER RAISES

BENEFITS

Increase shoulder strength.

TARGETS

Shoulders, upper back and trunk.

TECHNIQUE

The Front Raise challenges the trunk and front of your shoulders. The Side Raise targets your whole shoulder muscle (deltoid). Stabilize your trunk at all times and keep your posture neutral.

The key with these two exercises is not to shrug your shoulders. As you lift the weight, keep your neck muscles relaxed and gently hold your shoulder blades down and together. Pause, then lower the weights. Progress by increasing the weight and/or reps.

FRONT RAISE

START   **FINISH**

SIDE RAISE

START   **FINISH**

7 times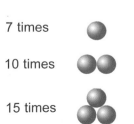

10 times

15 times

Bearing in mind....

...try on toes or with eyes closed.

OVERHEAD PRESS

START

FINISH

BENEFITS

Strengthen shoulder region while challenging correct sitting posture.

TARGETS

Shoulder, triceps and core.

TECHNIQUE

Start in a seated position. Bring the weights up to your shoulders, palms facing forward. Engage your TVA. Exhale as you press the weight slowly overhead by straightening your arms. The ball should remain motionless throughout the exercise as you maintain a neutral posture. Lower the weight.

The tendency with the Overhead Press, especially as you get tired, is to arch your spine and lean back. This should be considered cheating and unsafe! Keep your spine neutral; this is when you really challenge your core.

Increase the number of reps and/or the weight to progress.

Bearing in mind....

This is a great exercise to test whether your core muscles may be a weak link. If you cannot maintain a neutral posture, you need to train your core more than your shoulder strength. Do not pass Go. Do not collect $200. Go directly to Chapter 4...

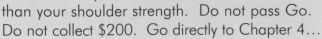

 8 times

12 times

 15 times

ABC'S

BENEFITS

Improve shoulder stability and control.

TARGETS

Shoulder.

TECHNIQUE

Hold the ball against the wall with a straight arm. Keep your shoulder blade completely still. Do not roll it forward nor pull it back so that it pinches.

In a slow and controlled manner roll the ball as you 'write' the letters of the alphabet.

Bearing in mind....

...the most important point for this exercise is to keep your shoulder blade still.

Letters A - H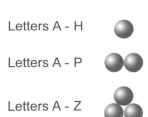

Letters A - P

Letters A - Z

START

MIDDLE

FINISH

BALL CHINS

START

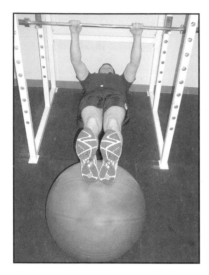

FINISH

BENEFITS

Improve upper body strength and core stability.

TARGETS

Upper back, low back, buttocks, hamstrings and arms.

TECHNIQUE

Lie on the ground with both heels on the ball. Grab onto a fixed bar or surface (or use a friend's hands!). Straighten your body so that the buttocks are in line with the feet and shoulders. The neck and back should follow this neutral spine. Pull up as far as possible. Squeeze your shoulder blades together and hold for a time count. Keep toes together and pointed up.

For an advanced version, lift one leg off the ball.

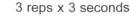

3 reps x 3 seconds

5 reps x 5 seconds

8 reps x 10 seconds

Bash, Bounce
& Balance

STANDING BALL BASH

BEGINNER

INTERMEDIATE

ADVANCED

BENEFITS

Exercises the whole body; balance, reaction and strength.

TARGETS

Core, shoulders and legs.

TECHNIQUE

Hug the ball against your chest. Bend at the hips, knees, and ankles with your feet wider than shoulder width. This is the 'power position' or the stance that gives you the best balance; i.e. it would be hard for someone to push you over...not that anybody would want to do that! Have your partner lightly tap the ball in unpredictable random patterns and with different levels of force. Your job is to remain in the power position....in other words, do not move! Remember to breathe normally.

To progress, hold the ball further away from your body, stand only on one foot, and/or have your partner bash the ball a little harder and faster!

 20 seconds

30 seconds

60 seconds

OVERHEAD BALL BASH

BENEFITS

Improve your balance, body awareness and shoulder stability.

TARGETS

Shoulders, trunk and legs.

TECHNIQUE

In the 'power position', with slightly bent elbows, hold the ball overhead. Because of the challenge to your shoulders, your partner should tap the ball with less force than for the Standing Bull Bash (previous page).

To progress, try the Overhead Ball Bash while standing on a single leg. Have your partner bash the ball quicker and with more force. For a really advanced version, try the Single Leg Bash while you hop from side-to-side on the same leg, or alternate jumps between the right and left leg!

BEGINNER

SINGLE LEG

20 seconds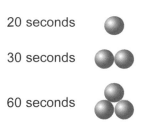

30 seconds

60 seconds

SHOULDER & HIP BALL BASH

SHOULDER

BENEFITS

Improve stablization of shoulder and hip joints.

TARGETS

Shoulder and hip musculature.

Bearing in mind....

...if this is too difficult, start on knees with elbow on ball.

HIP

TECHNIQUE

For either exercise the goal is to stabilize your shoulder or hip while your partner pushes the ball in an unpredictable way.

Try to keep a neutral posture at all times; shoulders back and down, chest out! For the Hip Ball Bash, maintain knees bent with arms out to the side for balance.

To progress the Shoulder version, place your feet further away. This increases the weight with which you lean onto the ball. For the Hip version, place more body weight on the knee that is leaning on the ball.

10 seconds

20 seconds

40 seconds

TABLE TOP BALL BASH

BENEFITS**

Increase static trunk strength and stability.

TARGETS

Trunk, TVA, buttocks and legs.

TECHNIQUE

Get into the Beginner position using the technique described for the Table Top exercise on page 46. The idea is to increase the challenge of this static exercise by having your partner 'bash' the ball. Try to use your buttocks and TVA muscles to stabilize. Do not let your hips sag towards the ground. Rest your head on the ball during this exercise.

To progress, try the Table Top Ball Bash with one leg raised straight out. Dinner is served!

BEGINNER

ADVANCED

10 seconds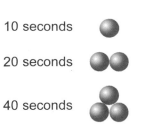

20 seconds

40 seconds

BRIDGE BASH

BEGINNER

BENEFITS

Increase static trunk strength and stability.

TARGETS

Trunk, buttocks, hamstrings and obliques.

ADVANCED

TECHNIQUE

Get into the Beginner position using The Bridge (see page 44). As your partner wallops the ball, focus on maintaining a neutral posture. Try to avoid droopy hips!

Progress by lifting one leg off the ball.

Bearing in mind....

...for all of the BASH exercises, you can increase the difficulty by closing your eyes. (Make sure you have a trustworthy workout partner...)

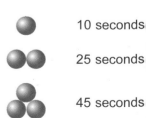

10 seconds

25 seconds

45 seconds

SITTY SITTY BOUNCE BOUNCE

BENEFITS

Build eccentric muscle strength. Learn how to bounce on the ball safely.

TARGETS

Abs, back, quads, buttocks and calves.

TECHNIQUE

Sit on the ball, spine in a neutral position, with your weight evenly distributed on each foot. Push explosively off the ground. Try to land on the center of the ball. Just as your feet land back on the ground, push again!

Start with small pushes, then progress to 'big air' as your abilities improve!

10 bounces

20 bounces

30 bounces

WHEELBARROW BOUNCE

BENEFITS

Challenge dynamic core stability and static arm strength.

TARGETS

Abs, hips, quads, calves, chest, back and arms.

TECHNIQUE

Lie on the ball. With the spine in a neutral position, hug the ball tightly! Push explosively into the ball with your chest. At the same time, push with your toes as your body starts to rise in the air. As you land, stabilize strongly and push back up again.

Be very aware of your back posture! If your hips sag with each bounce, you are not ready to perform this one, or you need to bounce more lightly.

Bearing in mind....

...maintain head posture please! This model was very tired and lazy!

 5 bounces

8 bounces

15 bounces

WALRUS BOUNCE

BENEFITS

Challenge dynamic core stability and upper body strength.

TARGETS

Chest, triceps, abs, hips, quads and inner thighs.

TECHNIQUE

This one is very difficult. You must be able to do at least 10 Advanced Push Ups (page 97) before you attempt this exercise. There are high loads placed on your wrists, so do not attempt if you suspect it may be painful. Place your hands on the ground in push-up position as you squeeze the ball tightly between your ankles. Push explosively off the ground with your hands. As you touch back down, absorb the impact by bending your elbows, then push up again! As you get better, try to lift the ball up as your upper body rises in the air.

Have a partner monitor your back posture! Do not let your hips or back sag. If they do, bounce more lightly, or wait until you have trained your core more.

3 bounces

5 bounces

10 bounces

Bearing in mind....

...back posture please! We fired the model after this project!

THE SKIER

START

MIDDLE

FINISH

BENEFITS

Improve coordination, balance, timing and explosive leg power.

TARGETS

Quads, buttocks, calves and core.

TECHNIQUE

The Skier requires good leg strength and a very good feel for the balance and movement of the exercise ball. You should be able to balance on the ball for at least one minute on your shins (see Look Ma, No Feet Part II on page 41). Once you are able to do this, you are ready to attempt The Skier.

Start with one shin on the ball and the opposite foot on the floor. Bend your knee and use this leg to push yourself up and onto the ball. Quickly transfer the push-off leg onto the ball and almost simultaneously stretch your other leg out to land on the floor. When this foot hits the ground, bend at the knee, then push back up the other way. Start slowly with the side-to-side motion, gradually progress to a more explosive pace and deeper knee bends as your proficiency increases.

5 times

10 times

20 times

SINGLE LEG TOE SQUATS

BENEFITS

Improve hip, knee and ankle strength and stability.

TARGETS

Quad, buttock, calf and trunk.

TECHNIQUE

This is an advanced version of the Wall Squat exercise (page 75). Keep a neutral spine and stable core. The idea is to perform a single leg wall squat only on your toes!

Do not let your buttocks move under or away from the front of your ball. Try to ensure that your knee always stays centered above the midline of your foot and does not move inwards toward your opposite leg as you squat down.

START

FINISH

5 times

8 times

12 times

TOP SPIN

START

BENEFITS

Improve dynamic core strength.

TARGETS

Trunk, obliques, abs, hips, quads, shoulders and chest.

MIDDLE

TECHNIQUE

Use The Hand-Stand (see page 49) to get you close to the Start position. Once you are in this position, raise one leg off the ball; this is your 'swing leg'. Keep the foot of the other leg, or 'pivot' foot, in contact with the ball. Slowly lower your 'swing' leg down to one side, trying to touch the ground.

Support yourself on the ball with the inside of your 'pivot' foot. As you bring your swing leg back up and over the ball, rotate your pivot foot so that the outside of that foot is in contact with the ball. Try and touch your swing leg to the ground on this side too! Once you do this exercise, you will realize that great trunk strength is required. Switch pivot legs after reaching your targeted rep number.

FINISH

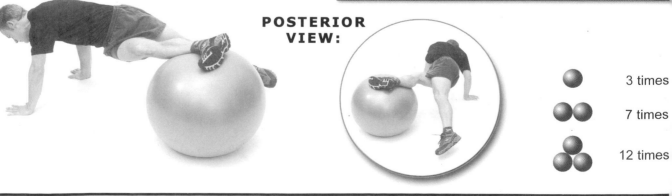

POSTERIOR VIEW:

3 times

7 times

12 times

BACK SPIN

BENEFITS

Improve dynamic core strength.

TARGETS

Trunk, obliques, buttocks, hamstrings and back.

TECHNIQUE

This is the upside down version of the Top Spin from the previous page. It is a little easier on the upper body, but still a great challenge to your trunk! Use the Bridge position to start this one out.

Choose a 'swing' leg and a 'pivot' foot. Lower your swing leg slowly to the ground while keeping your hips up. Do not sag! Try to touch the ground. Bring your swing leg back up and across your body, trying to touch the ground on the opposite side. If you rotate your pivot foot on the ball during this exercise, it will give you a better support and really challenge that leg.

Keep your palms face up to emphasize the stabilizing muscles of your upper back. Bring your hands closer to your side to increase the difficulty of the Back Spin!

LEFT

RIGHT

4 times

8 times

12 times

THE CYCLIST

START

BENEFITS

Improve dynamic control of core muscles, lower trunk and hips.

TARGETS

Abs, obliques, quads, hips, back, arms and lower leg.

MIDDLE

TECHNIQUE

This is a very advanced and strenuous exercise. Hold onto a chair or similar fixed object. Place your foot flat on the top of the ball with your knee up toward your chest. Lift the other leg off of the ground so that all of your weight is now on the ball. Slowly push the ball back, straightening your leg until only your toes are on the ball.

To return the ball to the Start position, pull your knee to your chest. Remember to exercise both legs.

FINISH

Bearing in mind....

...slight back rounding is okay for this exercise.

 4 times

7 times

12 times

THE SKATER

BENEFITS

Improve dynamic control of core muscles, lower trunk and hips.

TARGETS

Abs, obliques, quads, inner and outer hips, back, arms and lower leg.

TECHNIQUE

Hold onto a chair or similar stable object. Place your foot flat on the top of the ball with your knee up toward your chest. Lift the other leg off of the ground so that all of the weight is now on the ball. Slowly push the ball diagonally to the outside of your body until the inside of your foot is on the ball. Pull the ball back to the Start position. Now push out diagonally to the opposite side until the outside of your foot rests on the ball. Return to the Start position.

Do not forget to work the other leg. We advise you not to wear skates for this exercise…

RIGHT

LEFT

4 times

7 times

10 times

CATAPULT

START

BENEFITS

Improve coordination of the lower back and pelvis. Strengthen lower abs and pelvic muscles.

TARGETS

Abs, hips, chest and back.

FINISH

TECHNIQUE

Start by lying with your back on the ball. Hold onto an immovable object or partner. Slowly tuck your knees into your chest. Make sure your TVA remains contracted to prevent excessive back arching. Straighten one leg and lower it until parallel to the floor. Pull this leg back, pause, then extend the other one. This targets your hip muscles.

You can also try simultaneously extending one leg while the other is moving up to your chest. This shifts the focus onto your abs. To progress, extend both legs together; be sure to keep your abs and TVA contracted and your spine in a neutral posture.

▶▶▶▶ PROGRESSIONS

START   **FINISH**

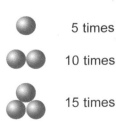

5 times

10 times

15 times

JOIN THE CIRCUS

BENEFITS

Improve balance, core strength and core stability.

TARGETS

The whole body.

TECHNIQUE

To get into the Start position, follow the instructions for 'Look Ma No Feet Part II' on page 41. Lift one arm directly overhead and parallel to the floor. Progress by doing the same with one leg.

Finally, you can do the most difficult version by lifting one arm and the opposite leg.

3 reps x 5 seconds

5 reps x 8 seconds

8 reps x 12 seconds

START

ONE ARM

ONE LEG

ARM AND LEG

WE HOPE
YOU ENJOYED
GETTING YOUR
BEARINGS!!

BALL BEARINGS

Ball Bearings Example Workout: BEGINNER 1

	EXERCISE	Set	DATE: Jan 01/04 Time / Wt	Reps	Time / Wt	Reps	Time / Wt	Reps	Time / Wt	Reps	Time / Wt	Reps	Time / Wt	Reps	Time / Wt	Reps
1	1 Legged Statue	1	5s	5 x												
		2	5s	5 x												
		3	5s	5 x												
2	Pelvic Shimmy	1	60s	-												
		2	60s	-												
		3	45s	-												
3	The Bridge	1	30s	-												
		2	30s	-												
		3	20s	-												
4	Crunches	1	-	15 x												
		2	-	15 x												
		3	-	12 x												
5	Back Extensions	1	-	15 x												
		2	-	15 x												
		3	-	15 x												
6	Superman!	1	5 s	5 x												
		2	5 s	5 x												
		3	5 s	5 x												
7	Wall Squats	1	3 s	10 x												
		2	3 s	7 x												
		3	-	10 x												
8	Hamstring Curls	1	3 s	10 x												
		2	-	10 x												
		3	-	8 x												
9	Chest Press	1	5 lb	15 x												
		2	5 lb	15 x												
		3	5 lb	15 x												
10	Shoulder Raise to the Side	1	3 lb	15 x												
		2	3 lb	12 x												
		3	3 lb	10 x												

NOTE: The above exercises, Times / Weights and Repetitions are EXAMPLES ONLY! If you are just starting your exercise program, get clearance from your Health professional first. Always start at a low intensity (a level that feels easy at first) and then gradually progress the exercises as you feel comfortable. If you experience any pain while, or after, performing these exercises, stop immediately and consult your Health professional.

Ball Bearings Example Workout: BEGINNER 1

DATE: Jan 01/04

#	EXERCISE	Set	Time / Wt	Reps
1	1 Legged Statue	1	5s	5x
		2	5s	5x
		3	5s	5x
2	Pelvic Shimmy	1	60s	-
		2	60s	-
		3	45s	-
3	The Bridge	1	30s	-
		2	30s	-
		3	20s	-
4	Crunches	1	-	15x
		2	-	15x
		3	-	12x
5	Back Extensions	1	-	15x
		2	-	15x
		3	-	15x
6	Superman!	1	5s	5x
		2	5s	5x
		3	5s	10x
7	Wall Squats	1	3s	10x
		2	3s	7x
		3	-	10x
8	Hamstring Curls	1	3s	10x
		2	-	10x
		3	-	8x
9	Chest Press	1	5 lb	15x
		2	5 lb	15x
		3	5 lb	15x
10	Shoulder Raise to the Side	1	3 lb	15x
		2	3 lb	12x
		3	3 lb	10x

NOTE: The above exercises, Times / Weights and Repetitions are EXAMPLES ONLY! If you are just starting your exercise program, get clearance from your Health professional first. Always start at a low intensity (a level that feels easy at first) and then gradually progress the exercises as you feel comfortable. If you experience any pain while, or after, performing these exercises, stop immediately and consult your Health professional.

Ball Bearings Example Workout: INTERMEDIATE 1

EXERCISE	Set	DATE: Jan 01/04 Time /Wt	Reps	Time /Wt	Reps	Time /Wt	Reps	Time /Wt	Reps	Time /Wt	Reps	Time /Wt	Reps	Time /Wt	Reps	Time /Wt	Reps
1 Look Ma, No Feet Part II	1	45 s	-														
	2	30 s	-														
	3	30 s	-														
2 Table Top	1	60 s	-														
	2	60 s	-														
	3	60 s	-														
3 Static Push-Up	1	30 s	-														
	2	20 s	-														
	3	20 s	-														
4 Side Bridge	1	30 s	-														
	2	30 s	-														
	3	30 s	-														
5 Ball Squeeze	1	-	15 x														
	2	-	15 x														
	3	-	15 x														
6 Ski Tucks	1	-	20 x														
	2	-	20 x														
	3	-	16 x														
7 Groovy Hips	1	-	20 x														
	2	-	20 x														
	3	-	20 x														
8 Hip Pointers	1	1 lb	18 x														
	2	1 lb	18 x														
	3	1 lb	18 x														
9 Curly Arms	1	8 lb	15 x														
	2	8 lb	15 x														
	3	8 lb	15 x														
10 Rear Shoulder Raise	1	5 lb	15 x														
	2	5 lb	15 x														
	3	5 lb	10 x														

NOTE: The above exercises, Times / Weights and Repetitions are EXAMPLES ONLY! If you are just starting your exercise program, get clearance from your Health professional first. Always start at a low intensity (a level that feels easy at first) and then gradually progress the exercises as you feel comfortable. If you experience any pain while, or after, performing these exercises, stop immediately and consult your Health professional.

Ball Bearings Example Workout: INTERMEDIATE 1

	EXERCISE	Set	DATE: Jan 01/04 Time / Wt	Reps
1	Look Ma, No Feet Part II	1	45 s	-
		2	30 s	-
		3	30 s	-
2	Table Top	1	60 s	-
		2	60 s	-
		3	30 s	-
3	Static Push-Up	1	30 s	-
		2	20 s	-
		3	20 s	-
4	Side Bridge	1	30 s	-
		2	30 s	-
		3	30 s	-
5	Ball Squeeze	1	-	15 x
		2	-	15 x
		3	-	15 x
6	Ski Tucks	1	-	20 x
		2	-	20 x
		3	-	16 x
7	Groovy Hips	1	-	20 x
		2	-	20 x
		3	20 x	20 x
8	Hip Pointers	1	1 lb	18 x
		2	1 lb	18 x
		3	1 lb	18 x
9	Curly Arms	1	8 lb	15 x
		2	8 lb	15 x
		3	8 lb	15 x
10	Rear Shoulder Raise	1	5 lb	15 x
		2	5 lb	15 x
		3	5 lb	10 x

(The table includes additional blank "Time / Wt | Reps" columns for recording further dated workouts.)

NOTE: The above exercises, Times / Weights and Repetitions are EXAMPLES ONLY! If you are just starting your exercise program, get clearance from your Health professional first. Always start at a low intensity (a level that feels easy at first) and then gradually progress the exercises as you feel comfortable. If you experience any pain while, or after, performing these exercises, stop immediately and consult your Health professional.

Ball Bearings Example Workout: ADVANCED 1

DATE: Jan 01/04

EXERCISE		Set	Time/Wt	Reps	Time/Wt	Reps	Time/Wt	Reps	Time/Wt	Reps	Time/Wt	Reps	Time/Wt	Reps	Time/Wt	Reps	Time/Wt	Reps
1	The Walkout	1	45 s	-														
		2	-	10 x														
		3	-	6 x														
2	Iron Cross	1	60 s	-														
		2	60 s	-														
		3	60 s	-														
3	Side Crunches	1	-	25 x														
		2	-	25 x														
		3	-	25 x														
4	Dolphin	1	-	20 x														
		2	-	20 x														
		3	-	15 x														
5	Ski Tuck & Twist	1	-	20 x														
		2	-	15 x														
		3	-	15 x														
6	Lunge	1	5 lb	15 x														
		2	5 lb	15 x														
		3	5 lb	13 x														
7	Calf Raises	1	-	30 x														
		2	-	30 x														
		3	-	27 x														
8	Push-Ups	1	-	25 x														
		2	-	20 x														
		3	-	15 x														
9	PullOvers	1	10 lb	20 x														
		2	10 lb	18 x														
		3	10 lb	18 x														
10	Flap Your Wings	1	5 lb	15 x														
		2	5 lb	15 x														
		3	5 lb	12 x														

NOTE: The above exercises, Times / Weights and Repetitions are EXAMPLES ONLY! If you are just starting your exercise program, get clearance from your Health professional first. Always start at a low intensity (a level that feels easy at first) and then gradually progress the exercises as you feel comfortable. If you experience any pain while, or after, performing these exercises, stop immediately and consult your Health professional.

Ball Bearings Example Workout: ADVANCED 1

DATE: Jan 01/04

	EXERCISE	Set	Time /Wt	Reps	/Wt	Reps	/Wt	Reps	/Wt	Reps
1	The Walkout	1	45 s	-						
		2	-	10 x						
		3	-	6 x						
2	Iron Cross	1	60 s	-						
		2	60 s	-						
		3	60 s	-						
3	Side Crunches	1	-	25 x						
		2	-	25 x						
		3	-	25 x						
4	Dolphin	1	-	20 x						
		2	-	20 x						
		3	-	15 x						
5	Ski Tuck & Twist	1	-	20 x						
		2	-	15 x						
		3	-	15 x						
6	Lunge	1	5 lb	15 x						
		2	5 lb	15 x						
		3	5 lb	13 x						
7	Calf Raises	1	-	30 x						
		2	-	30 x						
		3	-	27 x						
8	Push-Ups	1	-	25 x						
		2	-	20 x						
		3	-	15 x						
9	PullOvers	1	10 lb	20 x						
		2	10 lb	18 x						
		3	10 lb	18 x						
10	Flap Your Wings	1	5 lb	15 x						
		2	5 lb	15 x						
		3	5 lb	12 x						

NOTE: The above exercises, Times /Weights and Repetitions are EXAMPLES ONLY! If you are just starting your exercise program, get clearance from your Health professional first. Always start at a low intensity (a level that feels easy at first) and then gradually progress the exercises as you feel comfortable. If you experience any pain while, or after, performing these exercises, stop immediately and consult your Health professional.

Ball Bearings Workout Log

DATE:			Time / Wt	Reps	Time / Wt	Reps	Time / Wt	Reps	Time / Wt	Reps	Time / Wt	Reps	Time / Wt	Reps	Time / Wt	Reps	Time / Wt	Reps	Time / Wt	Reps	Time / Wt	Reps
EXERCISE		Set																				
1		1																				
		2																				
		3																				
2		1																				
		2																				
		3																				
3		1																				
		2																				
		3																				
4		1																				
		2																				
		3																				
5		1																				
		2																				
		3																				
6		1																				
		2																				
		3																				
7		1																				
		2																				
		3																				
8		1																				
		2																				
		3																				
9		1																				
		2																				
		3																				
10		1																				
		2																				
		3																				

NOTE: If you are just starting your exercise program, get clearance from your Health professional first. Always start at a low intensity (a level that feels easy at first) and then gradually progress the exercises as you feel comfortable.

Ball Bearings Workout Log

DATE:

EXERCISE	Set	Time / Wt	Reps	Time / Wt	Reps	Time / Wt	Reps	Time / Wt	Reps	Time / Wt	Reps	Time / Wt	Reps	Time / Wt	Reps	Time / Wt	Reps	Time / Wt	Reps	Time / Wt	Reps
1	1																				
	2																				
	3																				
2	1																				
	2																				
	3																				
3	1																				
	2																				
	3																				
4	1																				
	2																				
	3																				
5	1																				
	2																				
	3																				
6	1																				
	2																				
	3																				
7	1																				
	2																				
	3																				
8	1																				
	2																				
	3																				
9	1																				
	2																				
	3																				
10	1																				
	2																				
	3																				

NOTE: If you are just starting your exercise program, get clearance from your Health professional first.

Always start at a low intensity (a level that feels easy at first) and then gradually progress the exercises as you feel comfortable.